A Step-by-Step Learning Guide for Retarded Infants & Children

A Step-by-Step

Learning Guide for
Retarded Infants and Children

VICKI M. JOHNSON

ROBERTA A. WERNER

SYRACUSE UNIVERSITY PRESS   1975

Copyright © 1975 by SYRACUSE UNIVERSITY PRESS

Syracuse, New York 13210

All Rights Reserved

First Edition

All photographs courtesy of
Ms. Terry Holley

Library of Congress Cataloging in Publication Data

Johnson, Vicki M
        A step-by-step learning guide for retarded infants
and children.

        1. Mentally handicapped children—Education—
Handbooks, manuals, etc. 2. Perceptual-motor learning
—Handbooks, manuals, etc. I. Werner, Roberta A.,
joint author. II. Title.
LC4602.J62   371.9′28   75-22172
ISBN 0-8156-2173-6
ISBN 0-8156-2174-4 pbk.

Manufactured in the United States of America

PREFACE

The curriculum described in this book was developed to meet the educational needs of a diverse population of handicapped children. The curriculum was developed over a three-year period at the Sunshine Center for the Handicapped Inc., Knoxville, Tennessee, which is a private school for severely retarded and multiply handicapped children and adults. Since the student population at the Sunshine Center represents a wide range of age and ability levels, it was necessary to develop a curriculum which would serve many different individual needs. Rather than designing a single curriculum which was appropriate for a group of students, it was deemed advisable to develop many curricula, each of which was custom made to serve the needs of a single child.

For each child for whom a curriculum was designed, the determinant of the curriculum content was a list of answers to the question, "What skills does this child need to learn?" The skills identified as target skills for one or more of the children for whom curricula were developed included such behaviors as sitting unsupported, eating with a spoon, speech acquisition, grasping, visual discrimination, walking, and learning appropriate social behaviors. The target skills were categorized into the following types of activities: sensory stimulation, social behavior, imitative skills, gross motor development, self-care skills, language skills, fine motor skills, and perceptual abilities.

For most of the target skills, the process of skill acquisition was far too complex to attempt to teach the entire skill as a whole. It was necessary, then, to examine each target skill and to determine for each what subskills constituted the larger skill. In some cases, it was necessary to further reduce the subskills into more basic elements. From these basic elements of subskills, goal-directed behavioral tasks were identified. That is, each basic element of each subskill was considered as a behavioral objective, and learning tasks were developed which would accomplish that objective.

In all, 240 such learning tasks were developed. These tasks have been sequentially labeled from Task 1 to Task 240. The tasks have been categorized by the type of activities which they represent, and within each category the tasks have been ordered in sequence by difficulty level. For each task, a specific objective has been stipulated, the task procedure has been described, and the necessary materials (if any) have been listed.

The curriculum has been utilized at the Sunshine Center in various classroom settings and has proved to be a viable method for individual instruction within a group structure. The curriculum is also designed for use by parents, and ideally it may be implemented simultaneously by teachers in school and by parents in the home.

The underlying rationale for the development and utilization of this curriculum may be summarized as:

1. the belief that retarded children learn best if instructional components are reduced to the most basic elements and each of these elements is taught independently;

2. the belief that a task-oriented curriculum can be designed to provide for optimal individualization within a group setting if tasks are independently selected for each child to meet his or her specific needs; and

3. the fact that a task-oriented curriculum is a goal-directed curriculum in which each activity has a specific behavioral objective which is highly visible to parents and teachers.

Knoxville, Tennessee
Spring 1975

Vicki M. Johnson
Roberta A. Werner

CONTENTS

1 INTRODUCTION

The curriculum tasks included in this book were designed to meet the needs of a wide range of handicapped infants and children. The curriculum is appropriate in whole or in part for children between the ages of birth and twelve years. The major emphasis, however, is for children who have a functional level of less than four years of age. The curriculum is directly applicable for the following groups of children:

1. Infants between the ages of birth and two years who are moderately retarded or otherwise minimally handicapped.

2. Children between the ages of two and six years who are severely retarded or otherwise seriously handicapped. Some of these children may outgrow the curriculum presented here and move on to an academic preschool curriculum, while for other children this curriculum will continue to be appropriate.

3. Children between the ages of six and twelve (or more) years who are so severely retarded or so otherwise seriously handicapped that they are

functioning on an early childhood level in one or more areas of development.

The curriculum has been used with children of many age levels who have had a wide range of handicapping conditions. The following brief case studies provide examples of some of the types of children for whom the curriculum has been used effectively. These ten children were selected as examples because they represented various types of handicapping conditions and age levels and because they had made discernible progress while in the Sunshine Center program. There are many other children at the Sunshine Center who have similar records of accomplishment, and there are some children whose progress has been much more limited.

■ □ ■ □ ■ □ ■

BILLY P. was enrolled at the Sunshine Center in August 1970, at the age of five. His psychological and medical records indicated that he was a Down's Syndrome child with an IQ of 32. It was further noted that he had an estimated potential IQ of 37–42. He had a poor attention span and his speech was "limited to indistinguishable sounds." He had a very limited repertoire of manipulative and self-care skills and a serious perceptual disability which was attributed in part to visual impairment.

Billy was initially placed in the early childhood curriculum program, and he was later moved to an academic preschool curriculum. As of December 1973, at the age of eight, Billy could print all alphabetic letters and many simple words; he could read on a preprimer level; he had developed some concept of numbers; he could perform all self-care skills including dressing; he was socially adept; and his speech was very fluent and largely intelligible.

■ □ ■ □ ■ □ ■

LENNY D. entered the Sunshine Center in August 1970, at age five. Psychological and medical records at intake indicated a Downe's Syndrome child who had a short attention span and who had not responded to any items on an IQ test. The records noted that he was functioning in the severely mentally retarded range (20–35) and that "it is doubtful if he will ever be able to care completely for himself. A sheltered environment will be necessary." Follow-up examinations in 1971 and 1972 indicated IQ levels of 20–35, unintelligible vocalizations, and inability to manipulate a large crayon.

Lenny was instructed initially with the early childhood curriculum, and he was later transferred to an academic preschool curriculum. As of December 1973, at the age of eight, Lenny was able to read, to print, and to spell many words—including *windshieldwipers*. He was fluent verbally and largely intelligible and he understood simple number concepts. He was able to perform all self-care skills.

■ □ ■ □ ■ □ ■

SUZIE G. entered the Sunshine Center in September 1972, at the age of seven. Psychological and medical records at intake indicated that she had had a "cerebral concussion associated with cerebral palsy resulting in mental retardation." She had hydrocephalia shortly after birth and underwent an operation to insert a shunt. At intake, she was totally nonverbal; she wore leg braces and could not walk; she was not toilet trained; she could not feed herself, she could not use her hands to manipulate objects; she was partially blind; and she was profoundly retarded.

As of December 1973, Suzie could walk unassisted; she had an intelligible speaking vocabulary of twenty-five words; she could label objects and name people; she was nearly toilet trained; she could eat with a spoon, and she could perform many manipulative tasks.

■ □ ■ □ ■ □ ■

JOEY C. was admitted to the Sunshine Center in October 1971, at the age of five. He had a medical history of seizures, a broken arm at age five weeks, persistent choking on food, and poor physical condition. He was diagnosed in 1967 as a battered child. In 1969, he entered a rehabilitation program but he was released one year later when he had made no discernible progress. He was described as "refusing any kind of adult management, screaming, crying, and kicking." A follow-up examination in 1970 revealed that Joey was severely mentally retarded, that he had a vocabulary of two words, that he could not stand up without support, that he was not toilet trained, and that he "does not do anything for himself." At intake into the Sunshine Center, he was extremely thin with a distended abdomen; he wore a leather helmet to protect his head from banging or frequent falls; he had very poorly developed musculature; he could not stand unsupported or walk; he was withdrawn and unresponsive; the only sounds he produced were screams; he could perform no self-care skills.

As of December 1973, Joey could walk unassisted, feed himself with a spoon, follow simple instructions, and imitate some sounds. He could put together puzzles and perform many manipulative tasks. His tantrums had been eliminated, and he no longer wore his helmet. He was socially responsive and laughed quite readily. He was not yet toilet trained.

■ □ ■ □ ■ □ ■

MARILYN B. had a medical history of kidney defects, surgery as an infant, and involvement in an automobile accident at six months of age which resulted in a skull fracture, laceration of the brain, some nerve paralysis, and a left hemiparesis of both the spastic and rigid type. She entered the Sunshine Center in May 1973, at the age of two years. At intake she had a thumb-in-palm deformity of the left hand; she could not sit without support; she could not feed herself; she was not toilet trained; she was totally non-vocal; and she had no manual abilities.

As of December 1973, Marilyn could pull up to a standing position; she could sit without support; she could stand holding a railing for five minutes; she could feed herself with a spoon; she could use her hands to squeeze and shake; she was partially toilet trained; and she babbled and tried to talk.

■ □ ■ □ ■ □ ■

TODD S. entered the Sunshine Center in September 1971, at the age of three years. At entry, he was diagnosed as having severe motor retardation with a possible muscle disorder and with periodic paralysis. He could not walk; he was not toilet trained; he was nonvocal and made no attempt at communication.

As of December 1973, Todd could walk without assistance, feed himself with a spoon, imitate sounds, perform complex manipulative skills, and he was almost completely toilet trained.

■ □ ■ □ ■ □ ■

TINA T. was admitted to the Sunshine Center in June 1973, at the age of three years. Medical records at intake indicated that she had a history of Jacksonian type seizures, that she had a neuro-degenerative disease, and that her muscle tone was hypertonic. She lay with her legs in a basic infantile position (described as a "pithed frog position") with her knees bent and the soles of her feet touching. It was impossible to straighten her legs. She had no use whatever of her hands or arms, and her arms remained in whatever position they were placed in. She was unable to hold her head upright and was totally non-vocal. One statement in her medical records indicated that there was no hope for any improvement in her condition and that she could not be expected to do more than lie in the pithed frog position.

As of December 1973, Tina could grasp and hold objects; she could hold her head erect for brief periods; she had developed considerable strength in her right hand and arm and in her abdomen; she could pull to a sitting position with help; and she babbled some. Her legs could be straightened manually and they remained fairly straight when placed in that position.

■ □ ■ □ ■ □ ■

JACKIE W. was a brain damaged, battered child with an unknown degree of hearing and visual impairment. Pre-intake medical records indicated a severely damaged child who was rigid and spastic and unable to sit unsupported. He had good head control and was able to roll over but he did not use his hands for grasping. Jackie was admitted to the Sunshine Center in September 1973, at the age of fifteen months.

Three months after his entry into the Center, Jackie was able to sit up from a lying position; he could pull up part way to a standing position; he could side step around a playpen holding the sides; he could sit unsupported; he could creep; he could pick up and throw toys or otherwise manipulate them; and he could imitate some sounds.

■ □ ■ □ ■ □ ■

TOMMY T. entered the Sunshine Center in October 1973, at the age of 2½ years. Medical records indicated a history of seizures and delayed motor development and described Tommy as totally nonvocal, unable to walk, having only limited ability to hold his head up, able to crawl clumsily and generally "floppy in appearance." He made no effort to communicate either through sounds or gestures.

As of December 1973, Tommy had made noticeable progress in feeding himself and in toilet training; he babbled frequently; he pointed to things he wanted; he crawled with good control and he could hold his head up when in a prone position.

■ □ ■ □ ■ □ ■

WILLIAM L. entered the Sunshine Center in September 1973, at the age of nineteen months. At intake his medical records indicated that he was blind and probably deaf, that his physical development was one-third normal, that he had no head control, could not sit alone, and could not roll from back to front. He was on an exercise program which was directed by the Children's Rehabilitation Center and administered by his mother. After six months in the program it was reported that "it appears that William is not improving except for very small gains."

After four months at the Sunshine Center, William's legs had gained strength and he was able to push himself up on them. He was able to roll from back to front (and front to back), and he could hold his head up briefly while in a prone position. He played with and manipulated several toys and pieces of equipment.

2 SELECTING A CURRICULUM

The curriculum was designed for use in either an individual or a group instructional setting. If the curriculum is to be used in a classroom or group setting, maximum individualization can be achieved for each child within the group. The curriculum should be perceived as a pool of curriculum items from which many combinations of items can be selected to produce many different curricula. If curriculum tasks are selected independently for each child within a group, each set of tasks constitutes a separate curriculum for that child. If children are grouped by level of functioning, it is possible that some group members will have some curriculum tasks in common. It is unlikely, however, that a single set of curriculum tasks would be appropriate for each class member. Teachers, then, should select for each child those curriculum tasks which are appropriate for that child. Similarly, parents should select curriculum tasks that are most relevant to the needs of their particular child.

The first (and most critical) phase in the process of curriculum task selection is the determination of a child's present abilities. Before a teacher or parent can select an appropriate curriculum for an individual child, he or she must know precisely what the child can and cannot do at the moment. If teachers or parents do not define the child's abilities accurately, they may select tasks representing skills that the child has already acquired, thus delaying the child's acquisition of new skills. Conversely, if teachers or parents overestimate the child's abilities and assume that the child can perform skills which he or she in fact cannot perform, they may select tasks which the child is not yet ready to learn.

The checklist of behaviors on Table 1 is designed to assist in the determination of a child's abilities. There are 106 skills represented in nine categories. For each category, the teacher or parent (or both) should read each skill and determine whether the child can or cannot perform the skill. The column to the right of the skill description which is headed "Task Number" refers to the curriculum task number(s) dealing with the skill described. If the teacher or parent does not understand the skill description, reference to the appropriate curriculum task will be helpful.

The teacher and/or parent should read the skills listed in each category. When they reach a skill which the child is unable to perform, the task number of that skill should be marked as the appropriate entry point into the curriculum for that category. Since there are nine categories in all, there are nine separate curriculum entry points. The total curriculum for some children will consist of learning tasks from each of the nine different types of activities. An example of a curriculum for such a child is as follows:

    I. Gross Motor, Task 75 to 76
   II. Feeding, Task 86

III. Dressing, Task 106
IV. Toilet Training, Task 110
V. Grooming, Task 123
VI. Receptive Language, Task 139
VII. Speech, Task 154
VIII. Fine Motor, Task 205
IX. Perception, Task 219

For some children, it would be inappropriate to select tasks from each of the skill categories. If a child is very young or seriously handicapped, such skill areas as dressing, toilet training, grooming, or perception might well be inappropriate. A curriculum for an infant or a severely handicapped child might include only the following areas:

I. Gross Motor, Task 36 to 37
II. Feeding, Task 83
III. Language, Task 124
IV. Fine Motor, Task 163

TABLE 1   **Checklist of Present Abilities**

1. **Gross Motor**	*Does the Child:*	Task Number
	A. Move his or her limbs freely and frequently?	35
	B. Move his or her head from side to side?	36
	C. Raise his or her head when prone?	37
	D. Hold his or her head upright when sitting?	38
	E. Sit with support?	39–41
	F. Roll over?	42
	G. Raise his or her upper body when prone?	43
	H. Sit without support?	44–45

1. **Gross Motor**	*Does the Child:*	Task Number
	I. Move forward when prone?	46
	J. Make crawling motions when supported?	47
	K. Pull to a sitting position?	48
	L. Creep?	49
	M. Pull to a standing position?	50–53
	N. Sidestep?	54
	O. Stand without support?	55–58
	P. Take a step forward when pulled?	59–61
	Q. Walk with assistance?	62–66
	R. Walk without assistance?	67–69
	S. Climb stairs with assistance?	70
	T. Climb stairs without assistance?	71
	U. Descend stairs with assistance?	72
	V. Descend stairs without assistance?	73–74
	W. Alternate feet when climbing stairs?	75–76
	X. Have adequate large-muscle coordination and strength?	77–82

2. **Self-care: Eating**	*Does the Child:*	Task Number
	A. Make a sucking motion?	83
	B. Drink from a cup?	84–85
	C. Transfer food from hand to mouth?	86
	D. Transfer food from spoon to mouth?	87
	E. Eat independently with a spoon?	88
	F. Drink from a glass?	89
	G. Drink through a straw?	90
	H. Exhibit appropriate table behaviors?	91

3. **Self-care: Dressing**	*Does the Child:*	Task Number
	A. Pull up his underpants?	92
	B. Slide down his underpants?	93

TABLE 1   **Checklist of Present Abilities** (*continued*)

3.	**Self-care:**	*Does the Child:*	Task Number
	Dressing	C. Pull up outer pants?	94
		D. Slide down outer pants?	95
		E. Put on pants?	96
		F. Take off pullover shirt?	97–99
		G. Put on pullover shirt?	100–102
		H. Take off socks?	103
		I. Put on socks?	104
		J. Take off shoes?	105
		K. Put on shoes?	106
		L. Take off a button shirt?	107
		M. Put on button shirt?	108–109

4.	**Self-care:**	*Is the Child:*	Task Number
	Toilet Training	A. Toilet Trained?	110–118

5.	**Self-care:**	*Does the Child:*	Task Number
	Grooming	A. Wash and dry his or her hands?	119
		B. Comb and brush his or her hair?	120
		C. Wipe his or her nose?	121
		D. Blow his or her nose?	122
		E. Brush his or her teeth?	123

6.	**Language:**	*Does the Child:*	Task Number
	Receptive	A. Respond to sound?	124–125
		B. Respond to his or her name?	126
		C. Obey simple commands?	127–133
		D. Identify visible body parts?	134
		E. Manipulate body parts as instructed?	135

6. Language: Receptive

Does the Child: Task Number

F. Discriminate between two or more
different objects?   136–138
G. Manipulate objects as instructed?   139–141
H. Identify nonvisible body parts?   142
I. Follow instructions to "go to"?   143
J. Discriminate among similar
objects?   144
K. Follow two-part instructions?   145–146

7. Language: Speech

Does the Child: Task Number

A. Vocalize freely?   147
B. Imitate nonverbal cues reliably?   148–149
C. Imitate verbal cues reliably?   150–153
D. Produce words by combining
sounds?   154–156
E. Say words to label objects?   157–158
F. Respond to "what is this"?   159
G. Have a vocabulary of 25–50
words?   160–161
H. Use words in sentences?   162

8. Fine Motor: Grasping and Manipulation

Does the Child: Task Number

A. Reach for and grasp objects?   163–168
B. Hold and manipulate objects?   169–173
C. Move objects across the floor?   174–176
D. Push, pull, turn, squeeze, spin,
slide objects?   177–181
E. Use his or her thumb in opposition
to fingers?   182
F. Use a spoon to transport
substances?   183
G. Put objects in slots?   184–187
H. Stack objects?   188
I. Coordinate the use of both hands?   189–198

TABLE 1   **Checklist of Present Abilities** (*continued*)

8. Fine Motor: Grasping and Manipulation	*Does the Child:*	Task Number
	J. Hit one object with another?	199
	K. Turn knobs and open doors?	200
	L. Place objects in appropriate slots?	201–204
	M. Put lids and tops on jars and boxes?	202
	N. String beads?	203
	O. Pour liquids?	205
	P. Use tools?	206
	Q. Have adequate finger dexterity and strength?	207–213

9. Perception	*Does the Child:*	Task Number
	A. Put like objects together?	214–216
	B. Separate grouped objects?	217
	C. Do puzzles?	218
	D. Match objects to objects or objects to pictures?	219
	E. Group like objects (discrimination)?	220–222
	F. Match like shapes?	223
	G. Put objects into separate compartments?	224–225
	H. Match colors?	226
	I. Match pictures?	227
	J. Discriminate between objects by size?	228–231
	K. Match animal pictures with sounds?	232
	L. Match motor activities to auditory cues?	233
	M. Draw lines in stipulated relationships to objects?	234

9. Perception   *Does the Child:*   Task Number

    N. Play "Simon Says"?   235
    O. Put pictures of body parts together
        properly?   236
    P. Know "the same"?   237
    Q. Arrange objects to duplicate a
        pattern?   238
    R. Measure quantity?   239
    S. Recognize logical sequences of
        events?   240

In addition to the skill areas outlined above, all children, regardless of age or ability level, should have as part of their curricula tasks from the sensory stimulation sequence and the social behavior sequence. All but very young infants should also have imitation sequence tasks as a part of their curriculum.

The nature of a child's curriculum will be dependent upon the child's age and abilities and also upon his or her need priorities. If a child is two or three years of age and has no outstanding disabilities, the curriculum should include tasks from all curriculum areas with approximately equal emphasis on each. If, however, a child is four or five years of age and is not yet ambulatory, the curriculum should emphasize tasks from the gross motor sequence. The attainment of ambulatory ability should be considered a primary need priority for this child, who should spend a large portion of each day learning how to walk. Decisions about the distribution of tasks throughout a child's curriculum should be made independently for each child on the basis of his or her most immediate needs.

Curriculum tasks should be entered into a child's daily activities in a logical manner. Feeding tasks should be scheduled for snacktime or lunch-time; dressing tasks should be included as a part of toileting chores or coming or going from outdoors; gross motor tasks should be included in "free play" time; and language tasks can be incorporated into all daily activities. Here is an example of a daily sched-ule for a two-year old:

8:40–9:00 A.M.	Group Activities 1. "Good Morning Song" 2. Group game (Social Behavior, Task 24)
9:00–9:20	Snack 1. Pouring (Fine Motor, Task 205) 2. Separating plates, cups, napkins (Perception, Task 217) 3. Buttering bread 4. Table behavior (Feeding, Task 91)
9:20–9:30	Bathroom 1. Pulling down pants (Dressing, Task 93) 2. Use of potty chair (Toileting, Task 112) 3. Pulling up pants (Dressing, Task 92) 4. Washing hands (Grooming, Task 119)
9:30–9:50	Fine Motor 1. Task 184, three repetitions 2. Task 185, three repetitions 3. Task 187, three repetitions
9:50–10:00	Imitation 1. Task 31, Six behaviors with three repetitions of each

10:00–10:30	Language 1. Task 127 2. Task 132 3. Task 133 4. Task 134 (First two behaviors)

10:30–10:45	Fine Motor
	1. Task 183
	2. Task 200
	    a. busy box, three repetitions
	    b. surprise box, three repetitions

10:45–11:00	Imitation 1. Task 31, six behaviors with three repetitions of each

11:00–11:30	Free Play
	1. Task 81
	    a. crawl through tunnel
	    b. pull wagon
	    c. toss and catch a ball
	2. Task 82
	    a. log roll
	    b. board walk

11:30–11:35	Bathroom 1. Toileting (Dressing Tasks 92 and 93; Toileting, Task 112) 2. Wash hands (Grooming, Task 119)
11:35–12:00	Lunch. Same as for snack.
12:00–1:30	Nap
1:30–2:00	Music Class
2:00–2:30	Free Play 1. Gross motor, Task 77 2. Gross motor, Task 78

3. Gross motor, Task 81
    a. push wagon
    b. seesaw

2:30–3:00   Art
                 1. Sensory Stimulation, Task 6
                    a. soap snow

Once a child's curriculum has been selected and built into the child's schedule of daily activities, the curriculum tasks selected should be transcribed onto index cards. (In a classroom situation, the most efficient use of the total curriculum is to write all tasks on index cards and simply select cards for each child from the set.) An additional index card should be prepared for each child on which daily records of his or her performance can be maintained. An example of an appropriate record card is presented in Figure 1. Records of a child's task performance are essential to the updating and revising of the child's

Figure 1. Record card.

Name			Week			
Tasks	Reps	Mon	Tues	Wed	Thurs	Fri
(36)	10	xxxxx xxxxx				
(37)	10	oooox oxooo				
(83)	10					
(124)	10					
(163)	10					

curriculum. The child's curriculum should be reevaluated and revised as necessary, at least monthly and preferably weekly. When feasible, parents and teachers should review the child's progress together and work jointly to revise the curriculum.

3 IMPLEMENTING THE CURRICULUM

The effectiveness of an educational program is dependent upon two major variables: the quality of the curriculum and the teaching methods employed in implementing the curriculum. The second factor, teaching methods, is perhaps more critical than the first. Even if the curriculum is of exceptionally high quality, it will not be effective if it is implemented poorly. Since it is the teacher who brings the curriculum to the child, it might be said that for the child, the teacher and the curriculum are synonymous. That is, the teacher *is* the curriculum and everything the teacher says or does in the child's presence may be considered as part of the child's learning experience. The word *teacher,* as used here, refers not just to a classroom teacher but also to parents, paraprofessionals, and all persons who care for or work with the child.

The effectiveness of any teaching method is partially dependent upon the personalities of the teacher and the child. Methods which some teachers use very effectively may not be effective when used by other teachers, and, similarly, methods which are successful with one child may not be successful with another child. The teaching strategies used, then, should be selected on the basis of what works in a given situation. While there are no absolute rules of teaching methodology, some principles and practices are generally more effective than others. The remainder of this chapter contains brief descriptions of some of the teaching strategies which are generally effective with most retarded children.

Rewarding Appropriate Behaviors

A basic principle of behavior shaping is that if a child performs a behavior and experiences a positive consequence or reward for that behavior, the child will tend to repeat the behavior. Teachers, then, can influence a child's behavior by rewarding the child for certain behaviors. Behaviors which the teacher might want to encourage include performing a task correctly, following an instruction, sitting quietly, paying attention, vocalizing, or other such behaviors which are considered appropriate.

There are two types of rewards which may be used easily and effectively either at home or in the classroom: social attention and food. Social attention may be in the form of praise ("good boy"), a smile, a hug, holding the child, or giving the child a toy. Food rewards may be pieces of cereal, grapes, small bits of candy, raisins or other foods. The type of reward used should be selected for each child on the basis of the child's preferences. Some children do not like food but do respond to attention, while other children find food highly desirable but do not respond to attention. As a general rule, food and social attention should be used simultaneously. That is, the teacher should praise or hug the child at the same time the child is given a bit of food. This strengthens the rewarding effect of social attention so that when a food reward is not practical, social attention itself will be rewarding.

It is important that desirable behaviors be rewarded immediately and consistently. It is also extremely important that the child not be rewarded for inappropriate behaviors. Inappropriate or undesirable behaviors can be strengthened just as readily as appropriate behaviors if the child is inadvertently rewarded for them. Teachers (and parents) encourage the child to behave inappropriately without meaning to when they allow a child to have his or her way to terminate a tantrum or allow a child to eat a piece of food which has been stolen from another child's plate.

Ignoring Inappropriate Behaviors

A corollary of the principle of behavior shaping described above is that if a child performs a behavior and receives no rewarding consequences as a result of the behavior, the child will tend not to repeat the behavior. It is possible, then, to discourage or eliminate undesirable behaviors by preventing the child from receiving rewards as a result of a particular behavior. A child who is crying without apparent reason, screaming, having a temper tantrum, or otherwise behaving inappropriately should be ignored (and thereby unrewarded) rather than attended to (and thereby rewarded).

In order to effectively ignore an inappropriately behaving child, it may be necessary to remove the child from all probable sources of attention. As long as the child can see a parent or teacher or sibling or classmate, it is possible that the child might inadvertently receive attention. To be certain that the child receives no attention for inappropriate behavior, it may be desirable to leave the child in the room alone, to place the child in a chair facing the wall, or to place the child in a specially designated area isolated from other persons. In a classroom or a home, a screened-off area or a corner behind a bookcase might serve as areas to which the child can be removed.

Punishing Inappropriate Behaviors

Another principle of behavior shaping is that if a child performs a behavior and receives a negative consequence or punishment for that behavior, the child will tend not to repeat the behavior. The use of punishment in modifying the child's behavior is made necessary primarily by the fact that it is often impossible to prevent a child from receiving rewards as a consequence of a behavior. If one could effectively control all the rewards which a child experienced, punishment might never be necessary. However, some behaviors provide the child with powerful internal rewards which cannot be removed by ignoring them. For some children, such undesirable behaviors, as fixated finger play, hand-biting, stylized spitting, or eating dirt may produce very powerful and pleasurable sensations for the child. If these behaviors are ignored, the child continues to receive rewarding consequences as a result of the behavior itself. The teacher must intervene, then, to terminate the behavior physically and thereby terminate the rewarding effect. The termination of the reward itself, however, does not necessarily diminish the child's tendency to repeat the behavior. In order to discourage the child from repeating the behavior, it is necessary to produce a negative or punishing consequence.

The most effective procedure for the elimination of undesirable behaviors is to physically terminate the behavior (if possible) and at the same time punish the child by saying *"no"* loudly and firmly, by banging the table to startle the child, or by producing in some other way a movement or noise which is unpleasant for the child. The teacher should attempt to interrupt the undesirable behavior and punish it as soon as the child initiates the behavior.

Techniques which are effective as punishments will vary from one child to another. Such techniques as startling the child, reprimanding the child verbally, restraining the child physically, or removing a toy from the child are effective punishments for most children. More extreme punishment techniques such as corporal punishment (pinching, hitting, or twisting an arm) should be avoided. *Corporal punishment is dangerous both physically and psychologically,* and it is justifiable only in extreme circumstances. Punishments should be delivered while the child is in the act of performing the undesirable behavior.

Using Manual Guidance

Manual guidance refers to physical assistance which is given in order to help the child perform a task. A teacher uses manual guidance when putting his or her hands on the child's hands and physically manipulating the child's hands in such a way that the child performs the task. This technique is an excellent teaching method, and it should be used whenever possible in teaching a child a new skill. At the same time the teacher is guiding the child manually, the teacher should also instruct the child verbally as to how the task is performed.

On every occasion when manual guidance is used, the child should be made to perform as much of the task as possible, and all manual assistance should be withdrawn entirely at the earliest possible moment. If the teacher continues to provide more manual guidance than the child requires, the child may lose motivation to perform the task, and the child's efforts will decline.

Using Imitative Techniques

An imitative teaching technique is employed when a teacher performs a task and expects the child to imitate or copy the teacher's performance. Children may be taught to imitate through a series of systematic progressions described in Chapter 6. Once a child has become imitative, the child may learn many skills by watching a model perform them. For children who have developed the ability to attend to and imitate a model, the imitative technique may be an effective means by which to teach some skills.

Motivating the Child

The child should be consistently motivated to reach the outer limits of his or her capabilities. A child is motivated to act when he or she wants to attain a specific goal or objective. On seeing a toy across the room, the child may be motivated to move toward it; if thirsty, the child may be motivated to ask for a drink.

Some learning tasks have built-in motivations for a child. A child is motivated to shake a rattle because the child likes the sound produced; the child is motivated to turn the handle of a jack-in-the-box because the child wants to see jack pop up; and the child is motivated to pull the light string because the child wants to see the light come on. Other activities, however, do not have inherent motivations. For such tasks, the teacher or parent must provide the necessary motivation by encouraging the child to perform. In such cases, the child will be motivated if he or she knows that a reward is forthcoming once the child has completed the activity.

Parents and teachers often reduce a child's motivation inadvertently by intervening to assist the child in attaining the objective. If a child is given everything without having to ask for it, the child has no motivation to talk. If a child can go wherever he or she wishes by reaching up his or her arms to be carried, the child has no motivation to crawl or to walk. If a child is handed a nearby toy, the child has no motivation to reach for it. If parents and teachers are to extend a child to his or her fullest capacities, then, they must provide external motivation when necessary and they must also refrain from reducing the child's internal motivations to perform an activity.

Personality Factors

The teacher's (parents') general mode of behavior and self-expression can affect the child's learning. It is important for teachers to be extroverted rather than introverted in their behavior. Teachers should provide a stimulating verbal environment for the child by consistently describing ongoing activities, by singing, or by asking the child questions. Teachers should radiate enthusiasm for the child's activities and should use dramatic, exaggerated exclamations of praise or encouragement. Teachers should also be effusive in their demonstrations of affection and in their physical contacts with the child. A child will be neither motivated nor rewarded by artificial pats on the head or by mechanical statements of "good boy." The child can be highly motivated and greatly rewarded, however, by the teacher clapping his or her hands, smiling broadly, saying "GOOD BOY" with relish, and hugging the child warmly.

Home-School Cooperation

If a child is enrolled in a school program, parents and teachers should work cooperatively to educate the child. The child's learning will be greatly facilitated if the same curriculum and the same teaching methods are employed in both environments. Conversely, if teachers and parents have different sets of expectations and different standards of behavior, the child's learning will be adversely affected.

4 SENSORY STIMULATION

In the first two months of their lives, normal babies become aware of their environment. They look at and follow objects with their eyes; they are aware of people and respond to them with smiles; they attend to sounds; and they explore with arm and leg movements. As infants begin to show an interest in things around them, their parents respond to this interest by providing them with toys and by playing with them. Because infants take an interest in the toys and respond to the parents' attentions, the parents receive gratification for their efforts and are motivated to continue them.

In the case of retarded or handicapped infants, however, the situation may be somewhat different. As an infant the retarded child may not show much interest in the environment. The child may have difficulty focusing on objects or people and may appear not to notice them. The infant may be unresponsive to sounds and may make no effort to explore the environment. When the child's parents present a toy or play with the child, the retarded baby may make no response or show any indication of interest in the parents' attention. The parents, in turn, receive no gratification for their efforts, and they are not motivated to continue them. Because the baby seems content to lie quietly and appears disinterested in the environment, the parents may discontinue their efforts at stimulation. The retarded baby, then, may receive less environmental stimulation than does a normal baby.

Ideally, the retarded infant should receive more rather than less stimulation then a normal baby. Whereas the normal infant will actively reach out to explore the environment and seek stimulation, the retarded infant is apt to be more placid and less exploratory. If the retarded infant makes little attempt to impose him or herself upon the environment, parents and teachers must make an effort to impose the environment upon the child. Even if the child appears disinterested and unresponsive, a continuing effort should be made to stimulate the child. The tasks in this section are means by which parents and teachers can provide stimulation to the child's senses of touch, sight, hearing, and movement. These tasks are designed primarily for infants, but they are also applicable for young children.

TASK 1

Tactile

Objective:

Exploration of the environment through the sense of touch.

Task:

Place objects that are of various textures in the child's crib and playpen. Different objects should be fuzzy, smooth, silky, soft, or cuddly. Objects should be chosen which will attract the child's attention and motivate the child to touch or fondle them.

Materials:

Texture Ball—Creative Playthings
Snuggler—Creative Playthings
Clutch Ball—Creative Playthings
Baby Shapes—Creative Playthings
Terry Teddy—Your Baby Playthings

TASK 2

Tactile

Objective:

Exploration of the environment using the mouth as a sensor.

Task:

Objects should be available to the child which stimulate sucking, chewing, and biting. Use objects such as teething rings which can be easily washed and which are safe to chew.

Materials:

Space Rings—Creative Playthings
Teething Man—Creative Playthings
Three Teethers—Creative Playthings
Teething Jack—Creative Playthings

TASK 3   **Tactile**

Objective: *Task:*

**Exploration of   Cover a hot-water bottle with a terrycloth or
the environment   towel-like material and fill the bottle with
through tactile   warm water. Encourage the child to cuddle
perception of   or grasp the object
warmth and
softness.**   *Materials:*
                         Hot water bottle
                         Towel or terrycloth material

TASK 4   **Tactile**

Objective: *Task:*

**To explore and   Support the child in a sitting position and
play in water with   place both of the child's feet in a container
the feet.**   of tepid water. Encourage the child to kick
                         and splash in the water. Alternate using
                         warm water and cool water so that the child
                         experiences different temperatures.

TASK 5   **Tactile**

Objective: *Task:*

**To explore and   Place the child in a Baby Feeder or hold the
play in water with   child on your lap. Place a basin of water in
the hands.**   front of the child and encourage the child to
                         splash and play in the water using both
                         hands. Place one or two toys in the basin to
                         encourage the child to play. Alternate using
                         warm and cool water so that the child expe-
                         riences different temperatures.

TASK 6

Tactile

Objective:

To explore different types of substances and textures.

Task:

Provide the opportunity for the child to play in and with different kinds of substances. The child should be given the opportunity to explore the materials with any and all body parts. If the child exhibits fear of a substance or object, gradually bring the child into closer and closer contact with the substance while providing a reward for the child's approach toward the object.

Materials:

playdough
soap snow
water
sand
flour
finger paints

TASK 7 **Visual**

Objective:

To develop visual ability through visual stimulation.

Task:

Place within the child's field of vision objects that are colorful and that produce movement. When the child is in a crib, objects should be hung over the crib and on the sides of the crib. When the child is in a playpen, objects should be placed on all sides of the playpen.

Materials:

mobiles
hanging toys
moving toys (both those which are self-propelling and also those which the child can manipulate to produce movement)
colored lights

TASK 8 **Visual**

Objective:

To develop visual ability through a visually stimulating environment.

Task:

Place the baby's crib or playpen in a well-lit room where family activities take place. This should be done during the times of the day when the baby is awake and alert. Activity which takes place around an infant stimulates the child visually and encourages awareness of persons around the child.

TASK 9

Visual

Objective:

To gain self-awareness by looking in a mirror.

Task:

Place mirrors within the child's field of vision so that the child's reflection can be seen in the mirror. A plastic or metal mirror can be placed within the crib or playpen or glass mirrors can be placed outside the playpen.

TASK 10

Visual

Objective:

To focus on an object and to follow it with the eyes.

Task:

Place the infant on his or her back in the crib. Hold a flashlight or pen-light three feet from the infant's head. Turn the beam on and shine the light toward the infant's eyes. When the eyes focus on the beam of light, slowly move the light from left to right, up and down, and in a circle. The infant's eyes should move in the same direction as the beam of light. A toy or other object may be used in the same way.

TASK 11

Auditory

Objective:

To be aware of and to attend to sounds.

Task:

Place objects which produce sounds of different pitches, of varying degrees of loudness, or of definite types of rhythms in the baby's crib or playpen. Two types of objects should be used—those that are self-propelling and those which the child may manipulate to produce sound.

Materials:

music boxes
squeaky toys
clocks
phonograph records
toys which emit tunes when a string is pulled
rattles

TASK 12

Auditory

Objective:

To be aware of human voices and other household sounds.

Task:

Place the child's crib or playpen in the living area of the house so that the child may hear people talking, laughing, singing, answering the telephone, and otherwise producing sounds.

TASK 13

Objective:

**To receive
auditory
stimulation from
human voices.**

Auditory

Task:

A concentrated effort should be made by all
adults and children who are in contact with
the infant to stimulate the infant by cooing,
babbling, or talking. It is important to note
that children who are not exposed to auditory stimuli early will not respond to such
stimuli when they are available later.

TASK 14

Objective:

**To assume many
different body
postures during
the day.**

Motor

Task:

Change the body position by moving the
child from the stomach to the back and from
the back to the stomach and by holding the
child in a sitting position and in a standing
position several times each day. The infant
should also be taken from the crib and
placed in a playpen, on the floor, or in someone's lap several times each day.

TASK 15

Objective:

**To reach for or
move toward
an object.**

Motor

Task:

Dangle a toy or other attractive object near
the child and encourage the child to reach
for or move toward the object. When the
baby is lying on the stomach on the floor or
in the playpen, place an attractive object a
few inches from the child.

TASK 16

Motor

Objective:

To become increasingly aware of the hands.

Task:

Place a small mitten on one of the child's hands, leaving it there for a few minutes; then remove it and place it on the other hand. As a similar task, cut the finger portion of the mitten off so that the child's fingers are free. Place small objects near the child and encourage the child to pick them up. Repeat using the other hand. These activities will stimulate visual, tactile, and body awareness.

TASK 17

Motor

Objective:

To increase the child's awareness of movement of the hands.

Task:

Obtain a bracelet which has a bell or which jangles to produce a sound. Place the bracelet first on one of the child's wrists and then on the other. As the child moves the arms or hands, the bracelet should make a sound which attracts the child's attention and which is pleasing to the child. Bracelets may also be placed on both wrists simultaneously. Leave the bracelets on the child for ten or fifteen minutes each day.

TASK 18

Motor

Objective:

To increase the child's awareness of and movement of the legs.

Task:

Obtain bracelets as described in Task 17. Place the bracelets first on one ankle, then on the other, and then on both ankles simultaneously. Leave the bracelets on the child's ankles for ten or fifteen minutes each day.

5   SOCIAL BEHAVIOR

Broadly defined, social behaviors are any behaviors through which a child communicates with any other persons. In this sense, and of the child's behaviors observed by another individual are social behaviors, even if they are not intended as an effort toward communication or interaction. Put another way, behaviors may interfere with or prohibit interaction with another person and still be considered social behaviors. Social behaviors, then, may be either positive (fostering social interaction) or negative (deterring social interaction).

Social behaviors are often dichotomized as appropriate or inappropriate. The judgment as to whether a behavior is appropriate or inappropriate may vary from one parent or teacher to another and may depend upon the situation in which the behavior occurs or the particular child who performs the behavior. A behavior which is considered appropriate for a given child in a given situation might be considered totally inappropriate if done by a different child or the same child in a different situation.

Like most other behaviors, social behaviors are learned. A child is not born with a repertoire of appropriate or inappropriate behaviors. A child may learn a behavior initially through trial and error or by imitation or through some other means. When the child "tries out" a behavior for the first time, the child does not know what the consequence of the behavior will be. If the consequence turns out to be a rewarding experience, the child will repeat the behavior. If the consequence is not rewarding, however, the child will not be as likely to repeat the behavior. If the consequence is in some way unpleasant or painful for the child, it is even less likely the behavior will be repeated.

If a child incorporates a behavior into his or her daily life and performs it repeatedly, this in itself is evidence that the behavior produces rewarding consequences for the child. The rewarding consequences may come from within the child or from an external source. If the behavior is appropriate and the parent or teacher wants to encourage the child to continue to perform the behavior, the parent or teacher may strengthen the rewarding consequences of the behavior by providing additional external reinforcement for the behavior. If, on the other hand, the behavior is inappropriate and the parent or teacher wishes to discourage the child from performing it, the rewarding consequences of the behavior must be diminished. If the behavior is primarily supported by external rewards such as social attention or privileges, the parent or teacher may eliminate the behavior by removing the external rewards. But if the behavior is primarily supported by internal rewards (such as pleasurable sensations produced by the performance of the behavior) the parent or teacher must impose an external consequence which will neutralize or negate the internal reward. This may be accomplished by physical intervention to terminate the behavior as it occurs (and thereby terminate the pleasure produced), coupled with some event which is unpleasant for the child such as a loud noise, a sharp "No," or the removal of social attention.

The first task in this section, Task 19, relates to the elimination of inappropriate behaviors. This task is not a part of any particular curriculum sequence, and it should not be considered as an isolated curriculum task. The procedure described in Task 19 should be used consistently and continuously throughout all areas of a child's curriculum. The decision as to whether a behavior should be considered appropriate (or acceptable) or inappropriate (and therefore not acceptable) should be made both in terms of the child's current functioning and also with regard to the child's future circumstances. A behavior which is allowed to persist over several years is much more difficult to eliminate than a behavior which has existed for only a short period of time. Consequently, any behavior which may be appropriate for the child at the moment but inappropriate for the future should be eliminated now rather than later. Such behaviors as playing in food, spitting, twirling string, playing in the toilet, or pulling hair may be inoffensive behaviors when performed by infants or young children, but they become quite inappropriate as the child reaches school age. Also, most behaviors which the child performs in a fixated or highly stylized manner should be eliminated.

The remainder of the curriculum tasks in this section relate to a different dimension of social behavior. Tasks 20–28 represent activities which are designed to develop sociability or the ability to function appropriately in a social situation. Tasks 20–23 are designed for use with infants and young children, and their objective is to encourage the child to engage in play activities which include participation by another person. Infants can develop social responsiveness and begin to interact socially with adults and other infants when they are but a few months of age if they are provided the opportunity and encouraged to do so.

Tasks 24–28 are more sophisticated group activities which involve group processes and structured group relationships. These activities are designed for children who are enrolled in a school program, and they should be part of a child's daily classroom routine. It is suggested that these activities be incorporated into a "group time" period at the beginning of each school day. This period might also include the pledge to the flag, singing a "good morning" song, or other structured group activities.

TASK 19

Objective:

Elimination of all inappropriate behaviors as they occur.

Inappropriate

Task:

Watch the child closely for evidence of stereotyped, bizarre, or otherwise inappropriate behaviors. Such behaviors might include head banging, patterned arm waving, spitting, fixed staring, head rolling, or fixated finger play. To eliminate such behaviors, interrupt them immediately as they occur and prevent the child from performing them. At the same time, say "no!" sharply, bang the table to startle the child, or physically restrain the child for a brief period. When possible, an appropriate activity or behavior should be substituted for the inappropriate behavior. To eliminate inappropriate behaviors effectively, it is necessary that the behavior be interrupted at *each* occurrence. All persons who work with or care for the child should be alerted to immediately terminate the behaviors whenever they occur.

Note:

As a collateral task, the child should be attended to and rewarded for all appropriate behaviors.

TASK 20

Play

Objective:

To respond to people by laughing, smiling, or making sounds.

Task:

Hold the baby away from you and jostle him or her gently. Swing, bounce above your head, or draw the baby toward you. Laugh at the child and provide vocal stimulation. Watch for any sign of a response, hug and kiss the child, and repeat the "game" that caused the response. Try various means of play in order to get the baby to laugh or smile.

TASK 21

Play

Objective:

To engage in a play ritual which is initiated by the child.

Task:

Select an activity which the child enjoys and which is engaged in frequently. This may be scooting to a particular place, throwing a toy, banging an object, or holding a toy. Devise a means of making the activity a two-person game in which you participate along with the child. You might, for example, take turns banging the object or holding the toy, or you might return the thrown toy or return the child to the starting point after he or she scooted to a favorite place. Your intervention into the child's activity should be pleasurable, so do not persist if the child becomes frustrated or annoyed.

TASK 22

Objective:

To engage in a play ritual which is initiated by the adult.

Play

Task:

Teach the child to play peekaboo, hide the toy, "this little piggy," and other infant games. Impose yourself and your game on the child. Try your best to have the child attend to the game and respond to it. Stimulate the child by making excited vocalizations, squealing, and laughing. Reward the child for any participation in or response to the game.

TASK 23

Group Awareness

Objective:

**To be with,
to attend to, or
to respond to
other children.**

Task:

Provide the child with the opportunity to be with other children. Encourage him to watch and touch another child. Devise games or activities in which two children can participate. Reward and encourage any attention to or response to another child.

TASK 24

Group Awareness

Objective:

To take turns.

Task:

Give each child in a group five beads. Place a coffee can in the center of the table and explain to the children that they are going to drop one bead at a time into the can when their names are called. Call a child's name and assist the child, if necessary, to place one bead in the can. Proceed to the next child. Be sure that children drop beads only when their names are called and that they drop only one bead at a time. Give each child one turn before any child has a second turn. At first, go around the table in order, but after the children have learned the game the order may be varied. When all beads have been dropped in the can, reverse the procedure and have the children remove one bead at a time from the can.

This task may be varied by the use of such activities as putting pegs in a pegboard, stringing beads, or building block towers.

TASK 25

Objective:

To recognize the names of other children and to interact with them appropriately.

Group Awareness

Task:

Give each child a plastic margarine container and several beads (as many as there are children in the group). Explain to the children that they are going to give their beads to other children who will then put them into a coffee can in the center of the table. Give these directions: "I am going to call one of your names. Listen carefully and I will tell you whom you are going to give one of your beads to. Let's practice. John, give one of your beads to Mary. Mary put the bead in the can." Be sure to let each child give a bead to a different child at each turn so that each child will be required to recognize each other person in the class.

TASK 26

Group Awareness

Objective:

To interact appropriately in a group learning activity (color concepts).

Task:

Give each child a plastic margarine container and six beads, one each of the following colors: red, blue, yellow, orange, purple, green. In the center of the table place a coffee can. Explain to the children that they are going to place their beads in the can in the following manner. As you call one child's name and a color, the child must pick up the bead that is the color designated and drop it into the can in the center of the table.

Example: "Mary, put the blue bead in the can."

Be sure to give each child one turn before giving any of them a second turn. Mix up the colors that you label so the child must be able to recognize the color auditorily rather than imitate the previous child visually.

This task may be repeated using colored pegs and a pegboard or colored blocks to stack or colored beads to string.

TASK 27

Objective:

**To interact
appropriately
in a group
learning activity
(shape concepts).**

Group Awareness

Task:

Give each child a plastic margarine container and three beads of the same color but different shapes: one red round bead, one red square bead, one red cylinder bead. In the following manner, explain to the children that they are going to place their beads in the coffee can in the center of the table: "I am going to call one of your names and tell you which bead to place in the can. Listen carefully, so that you will know which bead to pick up. Mary, put the round bead in the can." When calling on the children do not call out the same shape two times in a row, but vary the order so that the child is required to process the label auditorily rather than imitating the previous child visually.

TASK 28

Group Awareness

Objective:

To interact appropriately in a group learning activity (shape and color concepts).

Task:

Give each child a plastic margarine container and a round, square, and cylinder bead of each of the following colors: purple, red, orange, green, yellow. In the following manner, explain to the children that they are going to place their beads in the coffee can in the center of the table: "I am going to call one of your names and tell you which bead to place in the can. Listen carefully, so that you will know which bead to pick up. Mary, put the RED, ROUND bead in the can."

When calling on the children do not call out the same shape and color two times in a row, but vary the order so that the child is required to process the label auditorily rather than imitating the previous child visually.

6 IMITATION

Young children learn a gread deal through imitating others. They watch an older child or an adult and they attempt to copy the behaviors which they have seen the model perform. As they grow older, children continue to learn by watching others even if they do not attempt to copy the model's behavior spontaneously or directly. Any time a teacher demonstrates an activity or shows the child how to perform a task, the teacher is expecting the child to engage in this process of observational learning.

Normal children generally become imitative at quite a young age, and they develop the inclination and ability to imitate without being specifically taught to imitate. Retarded children, however, are very often nonimitative either as young children or as they reach school age. If a retarded child never develops an interest in imitating others or the ability to learn from observation, the child's learning in all areas of development will be adversely affected. Retarded children, then, should be taught to imitate. Since the development of imitative ability in a young child can facilitate learning in many areas of development, the imitation-tasks sequence precedes the specific skill-development areas even though the initial task in the imitation sequence requires a higher developmental level than the initial tasks in some of the other sequences.

If a child is to imitate a model or to learn from observation, the child must first look at or attend to the model. The first step, then, in developing imitativeness is to teach the child to attend to the model when instructed to do so. The child may next be taught to imitate simple nonverbal behaviors and finally to imitate verbal cues. The imitation of verbal cues is directly related to speech development, and the speech sequence and the imitation sequence are in fact identical at some points. Since children normally acquire speech and add new words to their vocabularies through the process of imitating the speech of others, the development of speech in a retarded child can be greatly facilitated if the child has previously been taught to imitate reliably. It is suggested that the imitative sequence be included in a child's initial curriculum and that the sequence precede and then parallel many of the tasks in the speech and fine motor sequences.

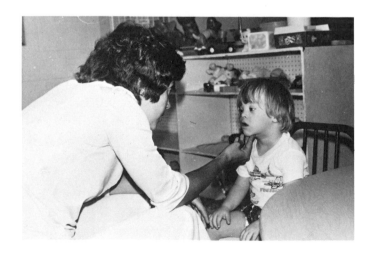

TASK 29

Attending

Objective:

To attend when told "Look at me."

Task:

Sit directly in front of and in close proximity to the child. Say "Look at me." If the child looks at your face, reward the child. If he or she does not look at you, repeat the instructions and hold a piece of food or other object in front of your face. If the child looks at you reward him. If he or she does not look, repeat the instructions, hold the food in front of your face with one hand, and with the other hand move the child's head so that he or she is looking at you. Provide a reward.

TASK 30

Nonverbal

Objective:

To imitate a simple nonverbal behavior.

Task:

Sit close to and face the child. Say "Look at me." As soon as the child looks, perform a simple motor task such as pushing a toy car across the table. Place the car in front of the child. If the child puts his or her hand on the car say "good." If the child pushes the car reward him or her with food. If the child does not touch the car, repeat your instructions, "Look at me," and repeat the task. Then place the child's hand on the car and assist him or her in pushing it. Provide a reward. Gradually demand a response which is identical to the cue before rewarding the child.

TASK 31   **Nonverbal**

Objective: *Task:*

**To reliably   Using the procedure described in Task 30,
imitate several   teach the child to imitate the following be-
behaviors.**   haviors:

> open the book
> put the block in the truck
> take the block out of the truck
> knock on the door
> stack two blocks
> put a lid on a box
> separate two cups
> touch your nose
> wave your hand
> clap your hands.

TASK 32   **Verbal**

Objective: *Task:*

**To imitate   Using the procedure described in Task 30,
mouth   teach the child to imitate mouth movements.
movements.**   These movements include:

> stick out your tongue
> open your mouth
> blow out a match
> round your lips

TASK 33   **Verbal**

Objective: *Task:*

To imitate sounds.   Using the procedure described previously, teach the child to produce sounds on cue. At first reward any appropriate mouth movements or any approximations of the correct sound. Gradually require a more perfect imitation of the sound. Sounds which may be used as stimuli include:

> AH
> OOOO
> EEE
> MMM
> p
> b
> c

TASK 34   **Verbal**

Objective: *Task:*

To imitate words.   Using the procedure described previously, teach the child to imitate one-syllable words. These words may be selected from among those which the child has previously attempted to produce (if any). Further verbal tasks which are performed imitatively may be found under the section on speech.

7 GROSS MOTOR SKILLS

In sequence, the gross motor tasks are designed for the development of the following skills:

1. head and neck control
2. sitting with support
3. rolling over
4. raising upper body when prone
5. sitting without support
6. scooting on stomach
7. pulling to sitting position
8. creeping
9. standing with support
10. sidestepping with support
11. standing without support
12. walking
13. stair climbing
14. ball skills
15. general muscular strength and coordination and physical fitness.

The tasks in this section are intended primarily for infants and young children. An underlying assumption of the gross motor curriculum is that retarded children learn motor skills in the same developmental sequence as do normal children, though perhaps at a delayed rate. The infant, then, should learn these skills in the sequence in which they are presented. In the gross motor curriculum more than in any other section, the acquisition of a particular skill is dependent upon the child's readiness, both in terms of prior learning and in terms of physical development. To illustrate, a child who has not yet acquired head and neck control cannot be expected to learn how to stand up. Neither should a four-month-old baby be expected to support weight on the legs. The teacher or parent, then, must be certain that the child is developmentally ready to perform a certain task before that task is included in the child's curriculum.

Although the gross motor section was written primarily for infants and young children, the curriculum is also appropriate for children who have grown beyond infancy without developing adequate gross motor skills. The walking sequence may be especially useful for older children who are as yet nonambulatory. In addition, Task 35, Task 69, and Task 80 provide special activities for children who have special gross motor needs.

TASK 35

Objective:

**To improve
flexibility
by stretching
connective tissue.**

Flexibility

Task:

The following exercises should be performed several times daily if the child is inflexible or is inactive. These exercises must be done gently and carefully. The use of too much force could cause serious injury.

1. Place the child on his or her back. Gently bend the child's knee and move it toward the stomach; straighten leg. Repeat with the other leg.
2. Place the child's arms at his or her sides. Move the arms out from the body and raise until the arms are above the head with hands nearly touching.
3. Place the child on his or her back. Slowly move the head from side to side.
4. Place the child in a sitting position. Massage the hands so that the fingers extend and contract.
5. Place the child on his or her back with the arms at the sides. Bend the child's arms and fold them across the chest.

Note:

If possible, a physical therapist or physical educator should plan an exercise program for each child geared to meet his or her specific needs.

TASK 36

Head and Neck Control

Objective:

To turn the head to the side.

Task:

Place the infant in the playpen or crib in a supine position. Using your finger or a feather, tickle the infant at one corner of the mouth so that the child will turn the head to the side of the face that is being stimulated. Repeat on the other side.

TASK 37

Head and Neck Control

Objective:

To raise the head while prone.

Task:

Place the infant in the playpen or crib in a prone position and kneel or stand in front of the child. Hold a light, a squeaky toy, or some type of stimulating object about one foot in front of the child and at eye level. Encourage the infant to raise his or her head by squeaking the object or moving the light.

TASK 38

Head and Neck Control

Objective:

To develop sufficient strength to support the head in an upright position.

Task:

Place the child in a sitting position and hold the child with one arm. If the child's head sags forward, return it to an erect position by tipping the body backward. Repeat whenever the child's head begins to sag. Perform this exercise for a few minutes several times each day.

TASK 39

Objective:

**To sit with
minimal support
in someone's lap.**

Sitting with Support

Task:

Hold the child in a sitting position on your
lap. Support the child's weight as necessary
by holding the child under the armpits. If
the child can maintain the upper body in a
fairly upright position without your assistance, merely provide the child with balance. The child should practice sitting in
this manner several times a day for several
minutes at a time.

TASK 40

Objective:

**To sit
independently
while propped.**

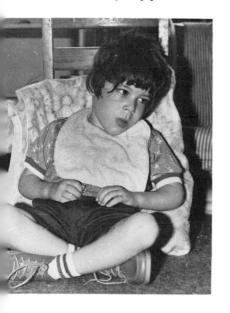

Sitting with Support

Task:

Place the child in a sitting position in the
playpen or on the floor. Place the child in
the corner of the playpen with a pillow behind his or her back or place two or three
pillows behind and beside the child if he or
she is on the floor. Place the pillows in such
a way that they provide the child with adequate support so that the child may sit this
way without assistance from you. Leave the
child in this sitting position for several minutes. Repeat several times each day.

TASK 41

Objective:

To sit unassisted in pieces of equipment which provide increasingly less support for the body.

Sitting with Support

Task:

The following pieces of equipment are sequentially arranged so that they require the child to provide an increasing amount of his or her own support. The child should be required to sit in a piece of equipment for five minutes without help. When the child is able to sit alone in one seat, move the child into the next piece.

Equipment:

1. automatic baby swing
2. baby bouncer
3. baby feeder
4. walker jumper
5. walker
6. high chair
7. tyke bike

TASK 42

Objective:

To roll from the back to the stomach, both to the left and to the right.

Rolling Over

Task:

Place the child on a mat on his or her back. Kneel beside the child's right side; reach across the child's body and place one hand on the left shoulder and one hand on the left knee. Gently pull the child toward you so that the child rolls to the right from the back to the stomach. Return the child to the back; kneel at the child's left side and repeat by pulling on his or her right shoulder and right knee. Gradually provide less assistance and require the child to expend an increasing amount of energy to pull him or herself over.

TASK 43

Raising Upper Body

Objective:

To support the upper body on the forearms.

Task:

Place the infant in the playpen or crib in a prone position. Kneel or stand in front of the infant. Hold a light, a squeaky toy, or some type of stimulating object about one foot from the child and three to six inches over his or her head. Encourage the child to support his or her body weight on the forearms and the lower portion of the body by squeaking a toy or moving a light so that the child raises up toward it.

TASK 44

Sitting without Support

Objective:

To sit in a chair without assistance.

Task:

Place the child in a small rocking chair or other chair with arms. If necessary, hold the child gently to help balance. Gradually withdraw your assistance so that the child is sitting independently. Place the child in the chair several times a day for ten or fifteen minutes at a time.

TASK 45

Sitting without Support

Objective:

To sit on the floor without support.

Task:

Place the child in a sitting position on the floor or in the playpen. If necessary, hold the child gently for balance. Gradually withdraw your assistance until the child is able to maintain balance in a sitting position.

TASK 46

Precrawling

Objective:

To initiate prone movement and to develop strength and coordination.

Task:

Place the child on a mat lying on the stomach. Try to get the child to move toward you by calling his or her name, holding a toy out of the child's reach, holding food in front of the child. At first, reward any attempt at movement. Gradually require an increasing amount of movement until the child is able to drag, scoot, or otherwise move 6–8 feet across the mat.

TASK 47

Objective:

**To maneuver
in a supported
crawling motion.**

Precrawling

Task:

Place the child on the stomach on a crawligator. Move the child's arms and legs in
such a way that the child moves the crawligator. Reward any attempt at movement.
Gradually reduce the amount of help given
and require greater efforts from the child.
Motivate the child by squatting in front of
the child, calling to the child, or by holding
a toy in front of the child.

Equipment:

Crawligator is manufactured by Creative Playthings. It is a small wheeled platform a few
inches off the ground. The child lies prone on
the platform with the hands and knees in contact
with the floor. Extra straps may be used to hold
the child's body on the platform.

TASK 48

Objective:

**To pull to a
sitting position.**

Pull to Sitting

Task:

Place the child on his or her back on a mat.
Hold the child's hands with your hands and
pull the child to a sitting position. Encourage the child to pull with his or her arms by
pulling slowly and keeping the child in a
bent-arm position. Gradually, require the
child to pull more while you do less of the
pulling. This activity not only teaches the
child to pull him or herself into a sitting position, but it is also an excellent exercise
through which to develop arm and ab-
dominal strength.

TASK 49

Creeping

Objective:

To locomote on hands and knees.

Task:

Place the child on a mat on hands and knees. Move a few feet away and call, wave a toy, or hold food out to the child. If the child makes any attempt to move toward you, provide a reward. Repeat. Gradually require the child to move a greater distance before providing the reward. The objective should be for the child to crawl several feet across the mat using a contralateral or left arm–right leg pattern.

TASK 50

Pull to Standing

Objective:

To move from a sitting position to a standing position.

Task:

Seat the child in a playpen facing the railing. Stand in front and hold the child's hands in yours. Gradually raise his or her hands so that the child attains a standing position. Reward. Return the child to a sitting position and repeat. Gradually withdraw the amount of impetus you provide and require the child to use the arms to pull him or herself into a standing position.

Note:

This task may be performed outside the playpen. Use of the playpen is suggested because further tasks in this standing sequence are performed in the playpen and performance of this task may generalize to subsequent tasks.

TASK 51

Pull to Standing

Objective:

To support the body with the hands on playpen bars and the stomach on a mat.

Task:

Place the child in a crawling position in a playpen and help the child to grasp the bars of the playpen with both hands. The child should support him or herself using the hands on the bars and the stomach on the playpen mat.

TASK 52

Pull to Standing

Objective:

To support the body with the hands on playpen bars and the knees on a mat.

Task:

Place the child so that the child is grasping the playpen bars with the hands and supporting the rest of the body with the stomach on the mat. Raise the child's hands upward on the bars until only the knees are in contact with the mat. The child should now be supporting him or herself by using the hands on the bars and the knees on the mat.

TASK 53

Pull to Standing

Objective:

To pull up from a kneeling to a standing position.

Task:

Place the child so that the child is grasping the playpen bars with both hands and kneeling on the mat. Raise the child's hands upward on the bars so that the child rises from the knees and assumes a standing position. The child should now have the hands on the top of the playpen railing with weight supported on the feet.

TASK 54

Sidestepping

Objective:

**To sidestep
around the
playpen to the
left and
to the right.**

Task:

When the child is able to stand independently by holding onto the top of the playpen, the child should learn to take sideways steps to the right and to the left. Stand at one corner of the playpen and call to or hold out a toy to the child. At first, reward any movement the child makes toward you. Gradually require the child to take several sliding steps before providing the toy or other reward. The child should eventually be able to walk completely around the playpen both clockwise and counterclockwise.

Note:

The child must learn to walk sideways before learning to walk forward.

TASK 55

Standing

Objective:

To stand with body weight supported.

Task:

Place the child in an upright position with feet on the floor. Hold the child under the armpits and provide support as necessary. Have the child support as much of his or her own weight as possible without the knees or ankles buckling. If necessary, place your feet outside the child's feet to prevent lateral sliding. Talk to and praise the child. Maintain the child in a standing position for 3–5 minutes per session and repeat the exercise several times each day.

TASK 56

Standing

Objective:

To stand with minimal support of body weight.

Task:

When the child can support most of his or her weight while standing, move your means of support from holding under the armpits to holding the child by the arms. Squat or stand in front of the child and hold the two arms to provide balance and minimal support.

TASK 57

Standing

Objective:

To stand independently by holding a stationary object.

Task:

Place the child in a standing position and place the hands on a stationary object. The child should hold or lean on the object as necessary for balance and support. Once the child has established a controlled stance, move away so the child is standing without human assistance. Objects for support may be:

1. bars attached to wall
2. desk or table
3. walker

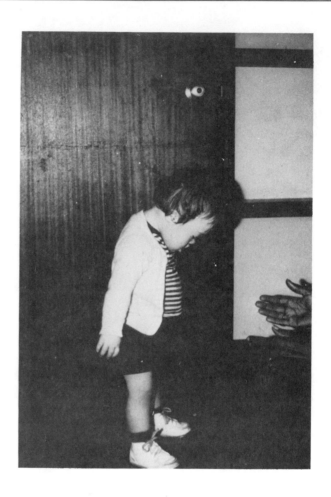

TASK 58   **Standing**

Objective: *Task:*

To stand unsupported with minimal balancing assistance.

When the child is able to support body weight while standing, remove all sources of support. Place the child in an open space and require the child to stand independently. Allow the child to hold your hand with one hand if necessary for balance. Gradually require the child to balance him or herself.

TASK 59

Walking

Objective:

To determine if the child is able to initiate a walking motion.

Task:

Have the child stand. Stand in front of and hold the child's hands in yours. Gently pull forward on the hands until the arms are outstretched. Continue to pull forward until the child is leaning forward and has begun to lose balance. Did the child take a step forward in an effort to regain balance? If the child took a step, bypass walking Tasks 60 and 61 and move directly to Task 62. If the child did not take a step, proceed to Task 60.

TASK 60

Walking

Objective:

To move the feet alternately forward in a walking motion with assistance.

Task:

Have the child stand. Stand behind and hold the child under the armpits. Place one of your feet behind each of the child's feet. Use your arms and feet as necessary to "walk" the child (push alternate feet forward with your feet). Talk to and praise the child as he or she walks.

TASK 61

Walking

Objective:

To walk with support from the back.

Task:

Have the child stand. Hold the child under his armpits from behind. Support the child as necessary while he or she walks. Do not move the child's feet for him or her. Praise and reward the child.

TASK 62

Walking

Objective:

To walk with front support.

Task:

Have the child stand. Stand in front of and hold both of the child's hands. Walk backward and lead the child. Provide support and balance as necessary. Be sure to hold your hands high enough so the child does not have to lean downward for support. Walk to a designated goal and reward the child when it is reached.

TASK 63

Walking

Objective:

To walk with non-human support.

Task:

Place the child in a walker or behind a small sturdy chair. Have the child walk by supporting him or herself on the object and pushing it along the floor. Call the child to you and reward the child for walking a short distance to you.

TASK 64

Walking

Objective:

To walk with support from the sides.

Task:

Have the child stand. Stand beside the child facing the same direction. Hold the arm nearest you just above the elbow. Walk the child, providing support and balance as necessary. Walk to a designated goal and reward the child when the goal is reached.

TASK 65

Walking

Objective:

To walk with minimal support from the side.

Task:

Have the child stand. Stand beside the child. Hold the hand (not arm) and walk the child. Allow the child to use your hand for balance but do not support or balance the child yourself. Walk to a designated goal and reward the child when the goal is reached.

TASK 66

Walking

Objective:

To walk independently using stationary support.

Task:

Have the child stand next to a wall using the wall for balance. Stand in front of and face the child; call the child to you. The child should walk to a designated place and be rewarded.

TASK 67

Walking

Objective:

To walk without support or assistance.

Task:

Place the child in the middle of a room or hallway or outdoors where there are no walls or objects to use for balance. Stand a few feet away and call the child to you. Reward the child for reaching you. Gradually increase the distance which the child must walk to reach you.

TASK 68

Walking

Objective:

To practice walking.

Task:

The child should walk unassisted (or with minimal guidance if still necessary) at least 200–300 yards every day. The child should walk wherever he or she goes in the course of a school day (to lunch, to music class, to physical education, to the bus, to the playground, etc.). In some settings, this will provide a good deal of walking. In other settings in which all activities are in close proximity, the child should be taken on walks to provide additional walking opportunities.

TASK 69

Walking

Objective:

To walk with the feet close together.

Task:

If the child walks with the feet spread apart or with the knees turned outward, the child should practice walking each day with the feet and legs together (within 8 inches). Place two 2″ x 4″ x 16′ beams on the floor set parallel and 8″ apart. Require the child to walk between the rails.

TASK 70

Objective:

To walk up stairs with assistance.

Stairs

Task:

Stairs should be at least 12″ in width and should not be more than 6″ in height from one step to the next. The stairs should have a railing and should be wide enough to accommodate two people side by side. Have the child hold the railing with one hand while you hold the other hand. Step to the next stair and pull the child up to you. If necessary, have a second teacher stand behind the child and manually guide the feet. Stay one stair above the child and require the child to hold onto the railing. Provide a reward when the child climbs a specified number of stairs.

TASK 71

Objective:

To walk up stairs unassisted.

Stairs

Task:

After the child can climb stairs fairly easily with assistance, begin to withdraw your assistance. Stand on the step just above the child, hold out your hand, and tell the child: "Go up the stairs." If the child does not have sufficient leg strength to step up, both hands may be used on the railing to pull him or herself up. Allow the child to place both feet on the same step and to lead with the same foot for each step.

TASK 72

Objective:

**To walk down
the stairs
with assistance.**

Stairs

Task:

Stand on the step below the child. Hold him or her with one hand; with the other hand guide the child's lead foot onto the step below. Guide the second foot onto the step. Reward. Repeat until the child is able to direct the feet onto the next step without assistance. Continue to hold the child and have the child hold the railing.

TASK 73

Objective:

**To walk
downstairs
without
assistance.**

Stairs

Task:

Stand just below the child on the stairs and call him or her to you. Hold the child's arm lightly, if necessary, but withdraw assistance as rapidly as possible. As the child becomes increasingly able to walk down steps unassisted, move farther away until the child must descend 5 or 6 steps before reaching you. Provide a reward when the child gets to you.

TASK 74

Objective:

To improve stairclimbing ability and to develop leg strength.

Stairs

Task:

Once the child is able to go up and down-stairs independently, these skills should be practiced regularly. In addition to providing increased ability, stairclimbing also provides an excellent exercise for leg muscles. The child should make several trips up and down the stairs each day.

TASK 75

Objective:

To lead with alternate feet when climbing stairs.

Stairs

Task:

Once the child can maneuver up and down-stairs unassisted, the lead foot should be alternated. Use manual guidance to indicate to the child which foot is to lead. Have the child step up with the right foot and bring the left up to the same step. For the next step, the child should step up with the left foot and bring the right foot up to meet it. Repeat several times each day.

TASK 76

Objective:

To alternate feet and avoid having both feet on the same step at the same time.

Stairs

Task:

Once the child has learned to alternate feet, have the child go in a continuous motion from one step to the next without stopping. If the child starts with the right foot, he or she will step up with the right, and then the left foot will bypass the step on which the right foot rests and move to the next step above the right foot. Completion of this task is the normal adult mode of stairclimbing.

TASK 77

Objective:

To develop eye-hand coordination and ball skills.

Ball Skills

Task:

Using a fairly large rubber playground ball, have the child perform the following activities:

1. Sit on floor with legs apart facing another child or teacher in same position. Roll ball back and forth using two hands with fingers pointed toward the floor.
2. Stand up holding ball. Drop ball on floor and catch it after first (or second or third) bounce.
3. Throw ball underhanded. Play toss and catch.
4. Kick the ball.

TASK 78

Objective:

**To develop
eye-hand
coordination
and ball skills.**

Ball Skills

Task:

Suspend to chest level a tether ball, a playground ball, or a whiffle ball. Have the child tap the ball with two hands whenever it swings toward him or her. Repeat the task with the child hitting the ball with the right hand only, with the left hand only, and with the right and left hands alternately.

TASK 79

Objective:

**To develop
eye-foot
coordination
and ball skills.**

Ball Skills

Task:

Suspend a tether ball or a playground ball from the ceiling so that it hangs three inches off the floor. Require the child to kick the ball each time it comes near his or her body. The child should kick with the right foot and then with the left foot so that the child becomes equally adept with each foot.

TASK 80

Objective:

To develop muscular strength, endurance, flexibility, and coordination.

Strength

Task:

If the child is nonambulatory or if physical disabilities prevent active play, the child should perform a series of physical exercises each day. The teacher should demonstrate and then provide manual guidance.

1. Sit-ups: With the knees bent and feet held down, the child lies on the back and rises to a sitting position.
2. Stretching: The child lies on the floor and the teacher sits facing the child. The teacher puts the child's feet flat against his or her bent legs, grasps the child's arms, and tugs forward so that the child bends at the waist. The child's legs should remain flat on the floor with knees straight.
3. Pull-ups: Attach a bar to a door frame or other support using rubber strips or springs so that the bar can be pulled downward through a range of 2–3 feet when sufficient force is applied. The child should stand or sit, reach the arms straight above the head and grasp bar, and then pull the bar down to chest level. Repeat several times.

TASK 81

General

Objective:

To develop muscular strength, endurance, flexibility, and coordination.

Task:

The child should participate in active play twice daily on the playground or in the playroom. Activities can include:

1. pull a wagon (empty or with another child in it)
2. push a wagon (empty or with another child in it)
3. run
4. play tag
5. ride a tricycle
6. seesaw
7. climb steps and slide
8. crawl through a tunnel (culvert pipe)
9. jungle gym
10. monkey bars
11. toss and catch with a ball
12. jump on a trampoline

TASK 82

Objective:

To develop body awareness, strength, and coordination through locomotor activities.

General

Task:

The child should perform a series of the following activities daily.

1. Crawling: Place three or more chairs in a straight line. Require the child to crawl underneath the chairs so that the stomach touches the floor.
2. Log Roll: Place the child on the back so that the feet are together, arms down at side. The child should roll the length of the mat so that the entire body rolls as one unit. The roll should be performed to the left and to the right.
3. Pushing: The child should stand and place the hands on the back of a light-weight chair. The child should push the chair from one side of the room to the other. Gradually increase the weight of the object to be pushed and/or decrease the height of the object so that eventually the child can push a cardboard box containing blocks or books across the room.
4. Pulling: The teacher should place a sheet or blanket on the floor of the area to be used. Depending upon the present strength of the child, place several heavy objects on the sheet and require the child to pull the sheet across the room. Gradually increase the weight of the objects.
5. Stairclimbing: Provide a set of stairs consisting of two steps and no railing. Require the child to ascend and descend the steps, first with the teacher's assistance and then without assistance.

6. Ladder: Place a ladder in front of the child so that the ladder is flat on the floor. Require the child to walk between the rungs of the ladder to the other end. As proficiency increases, gradually raise the height of the ladder.
7. Knee Walk: Require the child to "walk" down the mat on the knees with the arms at the sides or extended in front of the body.

8. Board Walk: Place a 2″ × 4″ × 6′–8′ board on the floor. Have the child stand on one end of the board and walk the entire length of the board without stepping off. The child should alternate feet rather than sliding one foot behind the other. After the child is able to walk forward without stepping off the board, repeat the activity with the child walking backwards, to the right side, and to the left side.

8   SELF-CARE

This chapter has been divided into four distinct self-care areas; feeding, dressing, toileting, and grooming. The applicability of each of these areas for a particular child will depend upon the child's age and ability level. The feeding sequence may be initiated with infants. The dressing sequence is not appropriate until the child has reached the toddler stage of development. The toileting sequence should not be implemented until the child has reached at least twenty months. In addition, the child must be capable of assuming a supported sitting position before using a potty chair. The toileting sequence is perhaps especially appropriate for those children who have reached the age of two years or more and have not yet been toilet trained. The grooming sequence is also dependent upon the attainment of an appropriate developmental level. Grooming skills should not be given priority in a child's curriculum until the child has developed the motor skills necessary to perform the tasks.

Since the four self-care areas are treated as independent sequences, it is conceivable that a child may have several self-care tasks simultaneously as a part of the curriculum. During the course of a day a child might, for example, work on an advanced feeding task, two beginning dressing tasks, a toileting task, and two middle-level grooming tasks. A younger child might, on the other hand, have only a beginning feeding task as a part of the curriculum.

The long-range overall objective of the self-care sequences is to enable the child to attend independently to basic daily needs. The attainment of the skills in these sequences will permit the child to achieve an increased independence in home life. In addition, attainment of these skills will provide the child with the abilities necessary to function appropriately in a school setting. Since some school programs require a child to be self-sufficient in terms of personal needs before they will accept the child into the program and since the class level on which a child is placed in a school program is often dependent upon self-care abilities, it is important that the child develop those skills before reaching school age.

TASK 83

Objective:

Sucking.

Feeding

Task:

In some infants, a sucking reflex is either nonexistent or very weak. These infants get milk from a bottle by thrusting their tongues outward and upward rather than by sucking. Tongue-thrusting babies can drink but they do not develop the ability to suck effectively. These infants can also eat soft food if it is placed on the back of the tongue (they do have a swallow reflex) but they do not chew.

Babies who continue to eat by tongue thrusting and who do not develop a strong sucking motion will encounter the following difficulties: they will not develop certain facial muscles and will therefore not have sufficient control to prevent drooling; they will not have sufficient muscular development and motor development for successful chewing and talking.

Some suggestions for developing a sucking response are:

1. Dip a pacifier in a soft food and give it to the child.
2. Place a small amount of soft food in the middle of the child's tongue.
3. Dab a small amount of soft food on the corner of the child's mouth.
4. Dab a small amount of soft food on the child's lips.

TASK 84

Objective:

To drink from a baby cup.

Feeding

Task:

Put juice or milk into a baby cup which has a covered top and a small drinking spout. Place the child's hands around the cup. Place your hands on top of the child's and raise the cup to the child's mouth. When the child has sipped from the cup, lower the cup to the table and repeat. Be sure the cup contains a liquid which the child likes. Gradually withdraw the amount of assistance provided until the child is able to raise the cup, drink, and return the cup to the table without assistance.

TASK 85

Objective:

To drink from an uncovered child's cup.

Feeding

Task:

Put a small amount of milk or juice into an uncovered child's cup. Assist the child in raising the cup and drinking from it and returning the cup to the table. When the child can drink from the cup without assistance and without spilling, gradually increase the amount of liquid placed in the cup.

TASK 86

Objective:

To grasp a bit of food with one hand and place the food in mouth.

Feeding

Task:

Use a piece of cereal, a small piece of candy, a baked bean, or some other food morsel that the child likes. Place the food bit in the child's hand and use your own hand to guide the child's hand to his or her mouth. Assist the child in transferring the food from the hand to the mouth, parting the child's lips if necessary. Gradually reduce the amount of help given. Be sure the child moves the hand to the mouth rather than moving the head to the hand.

TASK 87

Objective:

To transfer food from spoon to mouth.

Feeding

Task:

Place pudding, jello, or another food on a spoon. Have the child grasp the spoon by the handle with one hand and move the spoon into the mouth to eat the food. The child should be allowed to eat the food only after transferring it to the mouth using the spoon. Use a food which the child likes. Use manual guidance as necessary and then withdraw.

TASK 88

Feeding

Objective:

To scoop up food with a spoon and transfer it to the mouth.

Task:

Have the child hold the spoon by its handle with one hand. Place in front of the child a bowl which has in it a soft food which the child likes. Have the child use the spoon to scoop up the food and transfer it to the mouth. Use manual guidance. DO NOT allow the child to touch the food with the fingers. The progression for self spoon-feeding is:
1. A bowl containing soft food (mashed potatoes, pudding, applesauce, soft ice cream).
2. A flat plate which has soft food on it (pudding, applesauce, etc.)
3. A bowl containing loose food (beans, corn, peas, etc.).
4. A flat plate containing loose food.

TASK 89

Objective:

To drink from a standard container.

Feeding

Task:

Assist the child in drinking from the following containers. Gradually withdraw assistance and increase the amount of liquid placed in the container:
1. small soft plastic glass
2. juice glass
3. paper cup

Note:

If the child's hands are large and strong enough, the child should gradually learn to hold the container with one hand instead of two.

TASK 90

Objective:

To drink through a straw.

Feeding

Task:

Give the child a container of a favorite liquid. Place a straw in it and fix a similar container for yourself. Show the child how to drink through the straw and instruct the child to do so. Provide assistance if necessary by holding the straw and by molding the child's lips around the straw. If the child has difficulty in sucking the liquid the length of the straw, cut the straw to a length of four or five inches.

TASK 91

Objective:

To acquire appropriate table behaviors.

Feeding

Task:

Demand appropriate table behaviors. Do not allow the child to eat if the child is behaving inappropriately.
1. The child should sit in a chair at the table.
2. The child should not touch his or her food or the food of others with the hands (except his or her own bread, sandwich, etc.). It may be necessary to allow the child to "help" occasionally with his or her non-spoon hand for difficult foods like peas.
3. The child should not get up during a meal except in an emergency.
4. The child should not begin eating until a prescribed signal is given.

TASK 92

Objective:

To pull up underclothing.

Dressing

Task:

Place on the child loose-fitting underpants that have an elastic waistband. Before beginning the task, place the pants around the child's knee level. Issue a command to the child, "_____, pull up your pants." If the child fails to respond, repeat the command and help the child perform the task by placing your hands on the child's hands and pulling the pants up. When the child is able to perform this task, provide a reward and place the pants at the child's ankles.

Note:

It may be easier to teach the child to place one hand in front and one in back, rather than placing the hands on the sides of the pants.

TASK 93

Objective:

To slide down underpants.

Dressing

Task:

Place loose-fitting underpants that have an elastic waistband on the child. Issue a command to the child, "_____, slide your pants down." If the child fails to respond, repeat the command and help the child perform the task by placing your hands on the child's and sliding the pants down. When the task is completed, the teacher should verbally praise the child, using the same words each time so that the child will associate the praise with the performance of the task.

TASK 94

Dressing

Objective:

**To pull up
outer pants.**

Task:

Place loose-fitting pants that have an elastic waistband on the child. Before beginning the task, place the pants around the child's knees. Issue a command to the child, "_____, pull up your pants." If the child fails to respond, repeat the command and help the child perform the task by placing your hands on the child's and pulling the pants up. Provide a reward. As the child progresses the pants should be placed at ankle level.

TASK 95

Dressing

Objective:

**To push down
outer pants.**

Task:

Place loose-fitting pants that have an elastic waistband on the child. Issue a command to the child, "_____, slide your pants down." If the child fails to respond, repeat the command and help the child perform the task by placing your hands on the child's and pushing the pants down. When the task is completed, the teacher should verbally praise the child using the same words each time so that the child will associate the praise with the performance of the task.

TASK 96

Objective:

To put on pants.

Dressing

Task:

Seat the child on a chair or on the edge of a bed. Have the child grasp a pair of over-sized pants with two hands at the waistband. Have the child continue to grasp the waistband and at the same time bend forward until the legs of the pants are almost touching the floor. The child should then place one leg through the pants leg next to his foot. Repeat with the other leg. The child can then stand on the floor, bend over, and pull the pants up. Begin the task using short pants or underpants, and, as the child acquires the skill, progress to long pants.

TASK 97

Objective:

To take off a pullover shirt.

Dressing

Task:

Place an over-sized T-shirt on the child so that the shirt is over the child's head but both arms are free. Issue the command, "_____, take off your shirt." At the same time help the child grasp the bottom of the shirt and pull it over the head. Provide a reward.

TASK 98

Dressing

Objective:

To take off a pullover shirt.

Task:

Place an over-sized T-shirt on the child so that only ONE arm is through the sleeve of the shirt. Issue the command, "_____, take off your shirt." At the same time manipulate the child so that the child is learning to use the "free" hand to grasp the shirt by the bottom and pull it off the other arm. When the child can perform this task, repeat the task with both arms through the shirt sleeves.

Note:

Any responses which succeed in getting the shirt off the child should be rewarded.

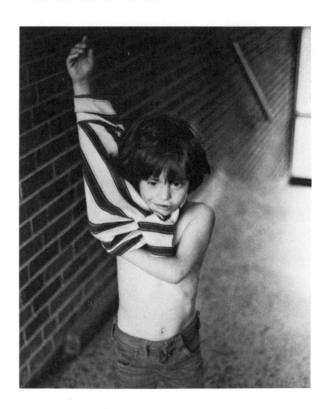

TASK 99

Dressing

Objective:

To take off a pullover shirt.

Task:

Place an over-sized T-shirt on the child. Issue the command, "_____, take off your shirt." Reward the child if the task if successfully completed. If the child cannot complete the task, assist the child. Repeat the task. If the child again cannot complete the task, return to one of the previous steps in the sequence.

TASK 100

Dressing

Objective:

To put on a pullover shirt.

Task:

Place an over-sized T-shirt through the child's arms and ask the child to pull the shirt over the head. Issue the command, "_____, put the shirt on." Help the child start the shirt over the head by taking the child's hand and grasping the neck of the shirt and placing it on the head.

TASK 101

Dressing

Objective:

To put on a pullover shirt.

Task:

Place an over-sized pullover shirt on the child so that the sleeves are at the child's elbow level. Ask the child to put on the shirt. Assist the child as needed.

Note:

Begin with a short-sleeved shirt and gradually work up to a long-sleeved shirt.

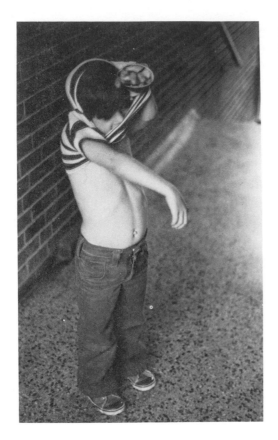 

TASK 102

Dressing

Objective:

**To put on a
pullover shirt.**

Task:

Place an over-sized pullover shirt flat on the surface of a table. Have the child stand facing the table and help the child place the left arm through the left sleeve and the right arm through the right sleeve. Then have the child poke the head through the neck opening and pull the shirt down. Provide a reward. Assist the child as needed and practice any parts of the sequence that the child has difficulty in carrying out.

TASK 103

Dressing

Objective:

To take off socks.

Task:

Place socks that are one size too big on the child's feet. Issue the command, "_____, take off your socks." At the same time, assist the child by taking the hands and grasping the top of the sock then pulling the sock downward off of the foot.

TASK 104

Dressing

Objective:

To put on socks.

Task:

Using socks that are one size too big have the child grasp the top of one sock with both hands. Issue the command, "_____, put the sock on." At the same time, help the child place the foot in the opening of the sock and pull the sock onto the foot.

TASK 105

Dressing

Objective:

To take off shoes.

Task:

Place the child's hand on the heel portion of one shoe. Teach the child to move his hand downward until the shoe is off the child's heel. When this is accomplished have the child slide the foot out of the shoe.

TASK 106

Dressing

Objective:

To put on shoes.

Task:

Select a pair of shoes that are at least one-half size too large. The shoes should be lace-up shoes that have a stiff heel. The teacher should loosen the lace on one shoe so that the opening for the foot is large enough for the child to easily slip the foot into the shoe.

Begin the task by placing the shoe on the floor in front of the child's foot. Issue the command, "_____, put your shoe on." At the same time help the child lift the leg and place the foot in the shoe opening. Provide a reward. Repeat the task withdrawing your assistance. When the child has successfully completed the task, have the child sit in a chair and give the shoe to the child. Issue the command, "_____, put your shoe on." At the same time place your hands on the child's hands and take the shoe down to the child's foot. Then help the child place the foot into the shoe opening. Reward. Repeat the task, withdrawing your assistance.

Note:

The child should become equally adept in putting on the left and right shoes.

TASK 107

Objective:

To take off a button shirt, coat, or sweater.

Dressing

Task:

Place a shirt with buttons on the child. Leave the buttons unbuttoned. Slide one arm of the shirt so that the child's arm is partially removed from the sleeve. Ask the child to take the shirt off. At the same time help the child use the free hand to remove the shirt. When the child can successfully remove one arm from the shirt, begin working on removing both arms from the shirt.

TASK 108

Objective:

To put on a button shirt, coat, or sweater.

Dressing

Task:

Use a shirt, jacket, or sweater which opens down the front. Unbutton or unzip the garment and open it up. Place the back of the garment on a table with the front of the garment facing upward. The neck of the garment should be on the edge of the table nearest the child who stands by the table. Issue the command, "_____, put on the shirt." Leaving the garment flat on the table, help the child put the left hand into the left sleeve of the shirt and the right hand into the right sleeve. (The child's arms should not be any farther into the sleeves than about the middle of the forearm). When the hands are in the sleeves properly, the child should swing both arms simultaneously up over the head. As the child does this the garment will fall on the body in proper position for wearing.

TASK 109   **Dressing**

Objective: *Task:*

**To put on a   Help the child hold a shirt by the shirt's
button shirt,   label using the left hand so that the inside of
coat, or sweater.** the shirt is facing the child. Manipulate the
                    child so that the right arm extends across the
                    body to the left side of the shirt. Ask the
                    child to place his or her arm through the
                    sleeve. After the child completes this step,
                    the shirt will be on one side of the body.
                    Then help the child bend the free arm at the
                    elbow and place it through the empty
                    sleeve.

                    Note:

                    Use verbal cues consistently through the perfor-
                    mance of this skill. The motor acts involved in
                    this will have to be practiced many, many times
                    before the child will be able to complete this act
                    independently. Be patient.

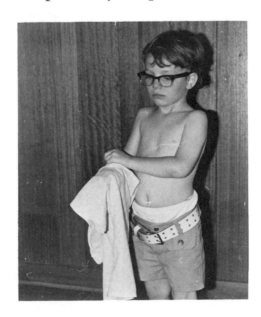

TASK 110

Toileting

Objective:

Task:

To involve the child's parents in the toilet training so that they may follow the same procedure at home.

Toilet training will be greatly facilitated if the same procedures are used both at school and at home. If possible, bring the child's parents into the school and show them the equipment and techniques being used. If personal contact is not possible, provide the essential information on the phone or in writing. Make an effort to enlist the parents in the training efforts.

TASK 111

Toileting

Objective:

Task:

For the teacher to pick up the signal that the child is about to begin or is in the process of defecating or urinating.

The teacher should prepare a chart and mark the time the child toilets daily. After a few days a pattern should be visible as children ordinarily toilet after waking, after eating, after playing. After the teacher establishes that a pattern is present, the teacher should study each child carefully to determine if the child gives any warning that he or she is about to urinate or defecate. (Some children bend over, have facial controtions, or become restless.) Whenever such a signal is given, place the child on the potty chair immediately. If the child does any elimination while on the chair, reward the child enthusiastically.

TASK 112

Toileting

Objective:

To produce a successful toilet on a potty chair.

Task:

If the child does not signal the need to use the toilet and if the child has not had a successful toilet on the potty chair after several trials, you may want to provide the child with assured success. Let the child drink two or three cups of juice or water. A few minutes later, place the child on the potty chair. When the child urinates, provide profuse praise and a reward. Repeat this procedure every 30 minutes if possible.

TASK 113

Toileting

Objective:

To sit quietly on a potty chair for 15 minutes.

Task:

Teach the child to sit on a potty chair. Remove the pants and place the child on the chair. While the child is sitting on the chair, praise and reward the child. Begin with a few seconds, and at every trial require the child to sit for a longer period of time until achieving 10–15 minutes. If the child cries on the chair, ignore the child. If the child does not cry, provide praise and a reward. Never remove the child from the chair while he or she is crying.

TASK 114

Objective:

To sit on the potty chair for 15 minutes out of every hour.

Toileting

Task:

Place the child on the potty chair for 15 minutes out of every hour. While the child is on the chair, stay nearby so you will be able to hear or see if the child toilets. It is important that you know immediately if the child is defecating or urinating. Use a clear glass receptacle so you can see or a tin receptacle so that you can hear. If the child toilets while on the chair, provide profuse praise and reward and remove the child from the chair.

TASK 115

Objective:

To ignore accidents.

Toileting

Task:

Whenever the child defecates or urinates in the pants, ignore the fact that the child has done so. Change the pants quickly with a minimum of social attention. The changing of soiled pants should NOT be a rewarding experience for the child.

TASK 116

Objective:

To develop a signal to indicate imminent toilet needs.

Toileting

Task:

Both nonverbal and verbal children must learn to provide the teacher and parent with a signal that indicates a need to use the toilet. For verbal children, the signal may be a single word (*potty*); for preverbal children, the signal may be a sound (*eee*); and for totally nonverbal children it may be a gesture (pointing to stomach). Once a signal is selected, pair that signal with the toilet experience. Perform the signal as you take the child to the potty chair; perform it again as you sit the child down; continue to perform it while the child is on the chair; and repeat it enthusiastically along with "good boy" or "good girl" and a reward any time the child produces the signal while on the chair.

TASK 117

Objective:

To use a regulation toilet.

Toileting

Task:

After the child has begun to use the potty chair regularly and easily, transfer the child to a regulation (but child-sized) toilet. If the child is fearful of the toilet, pair sitting on the toilet with rewards. Reward all successful performances.

Note:

The following skills should accompany the development of this skill:
1. pull outer pants and underpants down (Tasks 95 and 93)
2. sit on the toilet unassisted
3. pull outer pants and underpants up (Tasks 94 and 92)

TASK 118

Objective:

To develop independent toileting by chaining all the steps in the entire sequence.

Toileting

Task:

Initially when the child signals, take the child to the restroom, supervise the toileting, and return with the child. After many such trips, ask the child to go alone. If fear is exhibited, accompany the child, but gradually withdraw by standing farther and farther away from the toilet until the child is able to stay at the toilet when you are not in the bathroom. After the child is able to remain in the bathroom alone and complete the toileting sequence check on the child's behaviors occasionally to be sure that the sequence has been completed successfully. Reward all successful trips to the bathroom when the child returns to the classroom.

TASK 119

Objective:

**To wash and
dry hands.**

Grooming

Task:

Use techniques of manual guidance and imitation and reward correct performances.
Teach the skills in the following sequence
with each step as a separate task:

1. turn water on
2. test water for temperature
3. place hands under water flow
4. grasp bar of soap in one hand and rub
   soap on palm of other hand
5. replace soap in tray
6. rub palms together
7. rub right palm on back of left hand
8. rub left palm on back of right hand
9. place hands under water flow palms up
   and then palms down to rinse
10. turn off water
11. get towel from rack or dispenser
12. rub hands on towel to dry
13. replace (or throw away) towel

TASK 120

Objective:

To comb and brush hair.

Grooming

Task:

Use imitation and manual guidance and reward. Teach the child to comb and brush the hair by placing teeth or bristles against the scalp and moving the implement as appropriate for the child's hair style.

Equipment:

1. a very large-toothed comb for beginners and for children with long hair
2. a fine-bristled brush for children with very short hair
3. a medium-toothed comb for children with medium-length hair

TASK 121

Objective:

To wipe nose.

Grooming

Task:

Place the child in front of a mirror and give the child a kleenex. Guide the child's hand so that the hand containing the kleenex touches the nose, and then ask the child to wipe his or her nose. At the same time, physically manipulate the hand so that the child wipes the nose with the kleenex. When this has been done, ask the child to throw the kleenex away; take the child to the trash can; and help the child drop the kleenex into the can.

TASK 122   **Grooming**

Objective: *Task:*

To blow nose.   Place the child in front of a mirror. Take one
                        of his or her index fingers and place it under
                        YOUR nose and say, "blow" (gently blow
                        through your nose so the child can feel air
                        hit his or her finger). Then place the child's
                        index finger under his or her nose and say,
                        "blow." Reward if the child is successful. If
                        the child cannot complete the task, repeat
                        the initial step. When the child can perform
                        this activity, give the child a kleenex and
                        place it under his or her nose and ask the
                        child to "blow." The child should then
                        throw the kleenex away.

TASK 123

Grooming

Objective:

To brush teeth.

Task:

Use imitative and manual guidance techniques and rewards. Use the following progression, teaching each skill as a separate task.

1. get the toothbrush and paste from the holder (the child should be taught to recognize his or her own brush by color or by a distinctive marking placed on it by the teacher)
2. turn the water on
3. hold the brush under the water flow
4. take the top off the toothpaste
5. squeeze the toothpaste onto the brush
6. brush the teeth using up and down strokes
7. brush back teeth and insides of teeth
8. rinse the mouth
9. rinse the brush
10. turn off the water
11. put the cap back on the toothpaste
12. replace the brush and toothpaste on the holder.

9 LANGUAGE

The tasks in this language chapter have been separated into two independent sections—receptive language and speech. The tasks in the receptive language section consist of activities in which the child receives auditory signals and is expected to respond to them. These activities range in complexity from a startle response to a loud noise to following verbal instructions to go to the kitchen and bring me an egg. Since the receptive-language tasks require that the child be able to hear an auditory stimulus, they are not appropriate for deaf youngsters. It should be noted, however, that it is extremely difficult to diagnose auditory impairment in a young retarded child, and often infants who are presumed to be deaf are in fact unresponsive to sound for reasons other than deafness. It is therefore suggested that the receptive language tasks be included in a child's curriculum until there is definite evidence that the child is deaf.

The development of a receptive language ability is critical to a child's learning. If the child can attend to, process, and comprehend verbal instructions, the child's learning in all areas of development will be facilitated. The acquisition of receptive language ability should be included in the curricula of all infants and young children.

The sequence of speech tasks presented in this chapter may be initiated with young infants and followed through school age. Infants begin to vocalize by cooing or babbling when they are as young as one month of age. Their subsequent speech development depends in part upon the results of their early vocalizations. Infants who are rewarded for their vocalizing and encouraged to continue to vocalize are apt to develop speech abilities sooner than infants who receive no reinforcement for their early vocalizations. The process of transforming meaningless infantile noises into words is largely an imitative process in which an adult says a sound or a word and the infant tries to copy it. The development of speech will be facilitated if an infant has the inclination and ability to imitate. Since imitativeness must often be taught to retarded children, the development of imitative ability should parallel the speech curriculum.

The long-range overall objective of the language sequences is that the child will be able to participate effectively in a two-way flow of communication; that is, the child will be able to understand what is said and he will be able to make him or herself understood to others. If a child has a physical defect which interferes with the production of intelligible speech, it is suggested that a speech therapist be consulted. Parents and teachers can often improve the quality of a child's speech, however, simply by requiring the child to enunciate more precisely. Many times, if a parent or a teacher can understand what a child says, even though the quality is poor, the parent or teacher responds to the child without making an attempt to elicit better speech production. The child, then, knows that he or she has been understood and assumes that the speech production was adequate. If parents and teachers make it a practice to enunciate words clearly and request the child to reproduce them, the child will pay more attention to the quality of speech and make a greater effort at proper enunciation. Care should be taken, however, to avoid frustrating the child. Parents and teachers can also encourage appropriate speech by demanding speech rather than gestures as a means of communication. If a child can obtain everything desired by pointing or otherwise gesturing, the child has little motivation to talk.

TASK 124   **Receptive**

Objective: *Task:*

To determine if the child responds to sound.   Stand behind the child and produce a sound using a drum, bell, rattle, squeaky toy, or music box. Provide a reward if the child responds to the sound by blinking, smiling, a startle reaction, squealing, etc. Ideally, two teachers should be used for this activity, one to stand behind the child and produce the sound, the other to sit directly in front of the child to determine if a response was made and to reward the child for a response.

TASK 125   **Receptive**

Objective: *Task:*

To respond to and to locate a sound source.   The teacher should stand behind the child and produce a sound using a drum, a bell, rattle, squeaky toy, or music box. Provide a reward when the child turns toward the sound source. Gradually move farther away from the child and into different parts of the room, produce the sound, and reward the child for turning toward the sound source.

TASK 126   **Receptive**

Objective: *Task:*

To respond to his or her name.   Sit in front of the child and say his or her name loudly and clearly. Provide a reward when the child looks at you. Gradually move greater distances away from the child and say the child's name.

TASK 127

Objective:

**Proper response
to the command:
"Look at me."**

Receptive

Task:

Face the child with your face near the child's. Say, "John, look at me." If the child looks at your face, reward him (food, hugs, praise, etc.). If he does not look, repeat the command and simultaneously move his head with your hand until he is looking at you. Provide a reward.

TASK 128

Objective:

**Response to
the word *No*.**

Receptive

Task:

Isolate a behavior which the child exhibits frequently and which is an inappropriate behavior. The behavior should be one which the child can be physically made to stop. At every occurrence of this behavior, say *No* and stop the behavior. Repeat the word *No* continuously as you terminate the behavior. Gradually add a second behavior to be terminated and possibly a third. Examples of inappropriate behaviors which can be physically terminated:
1. child pulling his or her own or someone else's hair
2. child hitting him or herself
3. head banging

TASK 129

Receptive

Objective:

Proper response to the command: "Stop that."

Task:

Learning trials for this task can be conducted only when the child performs some action which is inappropriate. Select an undesirable behavior which may be physically terminated (child pulling the hair, screaming, biting himself, engaging in self-stimulatory behaviors with hands in front of face, etc.). When the behavior occurs, say, "John, stop that," and simultaneously terminate the behavior, by holding his hands still in his lap, for example. Reward. After several repetitions, say, "John, stop that," and give the child an opportunity to terminate the behavior by himself. If he does, reward him. If he does not, repeat the command and physically restrain him and then reward. When one behavior has come under the control of the command, select a second behavior. Continue to reinforce the termination of any behavior following the command.

TASK 130

Receptive

Objective:

Proper response to the command: "Give me the (object)."

Task:

Give the child a ball (doll, toy, block, etc.). Wait a short while. Then say, "Mary, give me the ball," and simultaneously hold out your hand. If the child reaches out the ball to you, take it from her and reward her. If she does not make an attempt to give you the ball, repeat the command and at the same time extend her hand toward you and take the object from her. Provide a reward. Use different objects.

TASK 131

Objective:

**Proper response
to the command:
"Put that down."**

Receptive

Task:

Give the child an object of any kind. Say, "Mary, put that down." If the child puts it down, reward her. If she does not put it down, repeat the command and at the same time manipulate her hands so that she puts the object down. Provide a reward. The objects used may be put down on the table, the floor, or the ground depending on where the child is seated.

TASK 132

Receptive

Prerequisite: Child is able to get up out of chair and walk a few steps.

Objective:

**Proper response
to the command:
"Come here."**

Task:

Stand a few feet away from the child (who is at first standing and later sitting in a chair). Hold an object which the child likes (food, juice, doll, toy, etc.). Say, "John, come here." If the child comes, give him the object and praise him. If he does not come, repeat the command while an aide physically maneuvers the child up to you. Gradually increase the distance which the child must travel to reach you until you are across the room from him.

TASK 133   **Receptive**

Objective: *Task:*

Proper response   Have the child stand by his chair. Say,
to the command: "John, sit down." If he sits down, reward
"Sit down."   him. If he does not sit down, repeat the com-
                           mand and simultaneously maneuver him
                           into his chair. Reward. As he learns to obey
                           the command, gradually move his starting
                           point farther from his chair until he starts
                           from across the room and on command walks
                           to his chair and sits in it.

TASK 134   **Receptive**

Objective: *Task:*

To touch the   Give the command, "Mary, touch
visible body parts   your_____." Simultaneously touch the ap-
on command.   propriate part on yourself. Use manual guid-
                           ance to assist the child as necessary. Reward
                           correct responses. Gradually withdraw imi-
                           tative and manual assistance. Ask the child
                           to touch the following body parts:

                           Tasks:
                           1. foot
                           2. arm
                           3. hand
                           4. finger
                           5. knee
                           6. toe
                           7. tummy
                           8. chest
                           9. thumb

TASK 135

Receptive

Objective:

To manipulate various body parts to perform tasks as instructed.

Task:

Issue instructions by saying, "John, _____your _____," and at the same time perform the task yourself. If the child performs correctly, reward him. If he fails to perform correctly, repeat the instruction, manually guide him so that he performs the task, and reward him. Gradually withdraw imitative and manual assistance.

Tasks:

1. raise your arm
2. wave your arm
3. hit the table with your hand
4. fold your hands
5. clap your hands
6. lift your leg
7. kick your foot
8. curl your fingers (make a fist)
9. open your fingers
10. open (and close) your mouth
11. close (and open) your eyes

TASK 136

Receptive

Objective:

To discriminate between two unlike objects and correctly follow the instructions: "Give me the _____."

Task:

Place two objects on the table in front of the child. The objects should be familiar to the child and they should not resemble each other in shape, color, or sound of the word which represents them. Examples: ball:cup, doll:shoe, box:pencil, spoon:ball. Point to each object and say the name of it. Then say, "Mary, give me the ball." Reward a correct response. If the child hands you the wrong object, say, "No. This [pointing] is the ball." Repeat your command and reward if correct. If the child does not respond correctly, remove the other object from the table and repeat the command. When the child responds correctly, replace the other object and repeat. Practice with different pairs of objects until the child responds reliably with six different pairs of objects.

TASK 137

Receptive

Objective:

To discriminate among three unlike objects and correctly follow the instructions: "Give me the _____."

Task:

Use the method described in Task 136. Put three objects on the table in front of the child and ask the child to give you one of them. Repeat with different combinations of objects until the child can consistently choose the items named.

TASK 138

Receptive

Objective:

To extend the child's receptive vocabulary by introducing unfamiliar objects for the child to select on command.

Task:

Use objects which the child is less familiar with than those used previously. Place two objects on the table and say, "John, give me the _____." When the child becomes consistent at identifying these objects, use three objects. Introduce new objects by pairing a new object with an old one and then replacing the old one with another new one. When the child has learned two new objects, add a third and place all these on the table at once. Gradually add new objects and increase the number which are on the table at once. Examples of objects: hammer, nail, key, glass, beads, ring, sock, toothbrush, bottle, can, flower, crayon, scissors, belt, string, fork, paper, soap, button.

TASK 139

Receptive

Objective:

To perform manipulative tasks involving two objects as instructed.

Task:

Provide the child with the two objects which are necessary for the task performance. Instruct the child to perform the task ("Mary, put the ball in the box") and reward her if she performs successfully. If the child does not perform the task, repeat your instructions and at the same time guide her so that she performs correctly. Activities which may be selected include:
1. put the doll in the bed
2. put the bead in the cup
3. put the book on the chair
4. put the block in the box

TASK 140

Objective:

To select the object named and manipulate it as instructed.

Receptive

Task:

Place three objects in front of the child. Instruct the child to perform a task using two of the objects. The child must select the appropriate objects and perform as instructed. Example: Give the child a ball, a car, and a box. Say, "John, put the *ball* in the box." If the child selects the wrong object (if he puts the car in the box), say "No, not the car. Put the *ball* in the box." This task may be expanded to require the child to select two objects from an array of four or five objects. Example:

1. doll, horse, box: put the *horse* in the box
2. marble, can, cup: put the marble in the *cup*
3. horse, marble, cup, can, box: put the *marble* in the *can*

TASK 141

Objective:

To increase the number of instruction-following behaviors.

Receptive

Task:

Using the same methods described in the previous tasks, teach the child to obey the following commands (or to perform the following behaviors when instructed to):
1. "John, throw the ball."
2. "John, kick the ball."
3. "John, push in your chair."
4. "John, put that in the trash."
5. "John, open the door."
6. "John, close the door."

Note:

Each of the tasks above should be practiced in sessions of three–five repetitions per session, and several sessions should be conducted each day. Once a command is obeyed reliably, it need not be practiced intensively, but it should be reviewed once or twice each day. Occasions for the exercise of many of these instruction-following behaviors will occur naturally in the course of a day's activities. On each occasion, the child should be required to respond correctly and should be rewarded for doing so.

TASK 142

Objective:

To touch nonvisible body parts on command.

Receptive

Task:

Give the command, "John, touch your _____." Simultaneously touch the appropriate part on yourself. Use manual guidance to assist the child as necessary. Reward correct responses. Gradually withdraw imitative and manual assistance. Ask the child to touch the following:

1. head
2. ear
3. eye
4. mouth
5. neck
6. nose
7. hair
8. teeth
9. tongue
10. back
11. chin

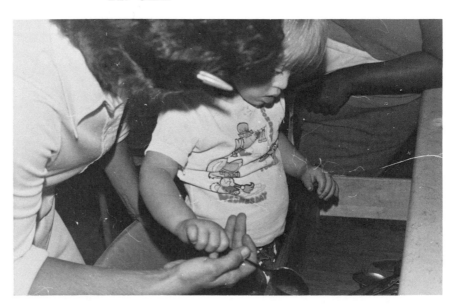

TASK 143

Objective:

To move from one location to another as instructed.

Receptive

Task:

Issue instructions by saying, "Mary, go to the _____." If the child performs correctly, reward her. If she does not perform correctly, repeat the instruction and at the same time walk her to the appropriate location. Provide a reward.

Tasks:

Go to the door.
Go to the window.
Go to the table.
Go to the coat rack.
Go to the bathroom.
Go to the classroom (from the hallway and then from farther away).

TASK 144

Objective:

To discriminate among several items and follow correctly the instructions: "Give me the _____."

Receptive

Task:

Object-identifications field trip. Take the child to a natural setting where several objects are housed together. Instruct the child: "John, give me the _____." Reward correct performances. For incorrect responses say, "No, this (pointing) is the _____." Then repeat your original instructions.

Trips:

1. Clothes closet ("Give me the _____," hat, coat, boot, shoe, pants, gloves, scarf, etc.).
2. Silverware drawer (spoon, fork, knife).
3. Toolbox (hammer, nail, screwdriver, saw).
4. Lawn (grass, leaf, stick, flower).

TASK 145

Objective:

**To carry out a two-part command involving:
(1) going to and
(2) bringing.**

Receptive

Task:

Instruct the child by saying, "John, go to the _____ and bring me a _____." If the child performs correctly, reward him. If he does not perform correctly, repeat the first part of the command and guide him to the appropriate location. Then repeat the second part of the command and guide him through it. Next, repeat the whole command and guide him through the whole performance. Provide a reward. Gradually withdraw manual guidance.

Tasks:

1. Go to the toybox and bring me a ball.
2. Go to the bookcase and bring me a book.
3. Go to the window (shelf) and bring me the box.
4. Go to the coat rack and bring me your coat.
5. Go to the cupboard (marked with an identifying X if more than one cupboard) and bring me a cup.

TASK 146

Receptive

Objective:

To follow two-part directions which require retention over a period of a minute or more.

Task:

Give the child a two-part instruction which requires the child to leave the room, go to another part of the building, and return. For example, "John, go to the kitchen and bring me a fork." Provide a reward.

Directions:

1. Go to the bathroom and bring me a towel.
2. "   "   "   playroom   "   "   "   "   beanbag.
3. "   "   "   kitchen   "   "   "   "   plate.
4. "   "   "   kitchen   "   "   "   an egg.
5. "   "   "   kitchen   "   "   "   a glass of water.
6. Go outside and bring me a leaf.
7. "   outside   "   "   "   "   stick.

Note Nos. 3–5: The cook's cooperation should be solicited. Children may find some items themselves, while they will need to ask the cook for others.

TASK 147   **Speech**

Objective: *Task:*

To encourage the child to make any vocalization other than crying.   Reinforce all sounds produced other than crying. When the child makes sounds of cooing, chattering, babbling, or other nonsense sounds, provide a reward. "Talk" back to the child, tickle, hug, or interact with the child in some way.

TASK 148   **Speech**

Objective: *Task:*

To develop imitativeness. The child should be able to imitate twenty-five simple motor behaviors.   Refer to the section on imitation (Tasks 29–34). The imitative sequence should precede and then parallel the speech sequence.

TASK 149   **Speech**

Objective: *Task:*

To perform fine motor exercises of the mouth and tongue by imitation of a model.   Using the imitative technique previously established (Tasks 29–34), require the child to perform the following:
1. Open and close mouth.
2. Round lips, protrude, and retract.
3. Move tongue from side to side, in and out, up and down.
4. Blow on objects (lips rounded):
   a. a kleenex   c. a hand
   b. a pinwheel   d. a lighted candle

TASK 150

Objective:

To bring child's sound productions under imitative control.

Speech

Task:

Imitate the child's sounds. When the child produces a sound, repeat it back. If the child then reproduces the sound following your production, reward the child enthusiastically with hugs, praise, food, etc. For example, Child: "bah-bah." Teacher: "bah-bah." Child: "bah-bah." Provide a reward.

TASK 151

Objective:

To bring the child's sound productions under imitative control.

Speech

Task:

Choose a sound which you have previously heard the child produce fairly frequently. Hold the child by the shoulders, put your face near the child's face, look directly at him and say "(Name) say (sound)." ("David say *eee*."). If the child produces that sound, reward him enthusiastically. If he does not produce a sound, repeat your command. With some children it may be necessary to begin by rewarding *any* sound which follows your command and gradually requiring closer approximations to the stimulus sound.

TASK 152

Objective:

To extend the child's repertoire of sound imitation to ten sounds.

Speech

Task:

Once the child has learned to produce one sound on command (see Task 151), other sounds should be brought under control using the same method. Repeat Task 151 with ten sounds which the child produces.

TASK 153

Speech

Objective:

To produce sounds which the child has not produced previously.

Task:

Define a target sound which is a combination of two sounds that the child frequently produces (such as *ba* and *eee* and *beee*). Use the imitative procedure described in Task 151. When one new sound is mastered, introduce a second new sound. Repeat with as many new sounds as possible or practical.

TASK 154

Speech

Objective:

To produce words by combining previously learned sounds.

Task:

Combine two sounds which the child can produce which make a word (such as $k + eee = key$; $ma + ma = mama$; $bah + l = ball$). Use the imitative procedure to elicit the word from the child. In addition, hold the object which the word represents in front of the child while presenting the stimulus. When the child produces the word, give the child the object (or picture of it if necessary, as in mama) along with the other rewards (praise, cereal, hugs, etc.).

TASK 155

Speech

Objective:

To extend the child's sound production to words.

Task:

Use the method described in Task 151. As a child masters or nearly masters one word, add another word to the training session. Add new sounds as necessary to form new words. Word-object combinations might include: cup, car, bean, toy, juice, pig, food, toast, bell, cow, milk.

TASK 156

Speech

Objective:

To produce two-syllable words.

Task:

Use the procedure described in Task 154. Combine syllables to form two-syllable words, such as puppy, candy, pepsi, baby, child's name or names of other students (use pictures or the objects presented upon production of the word).

TASK 157

Speech

Objective:

To label foods and table utensils.

Task:

Every meal should be a language class. Children should be required to label each of the foods they eat and all utensils used. Begin by providing labels and having child repeat. Gradually progress to providing stimulus "What is this?" and requiring child to respond with correct label. Labels will include: plate, fork, knife, spoon, cup, pitcher, tray, napkin, juice, toast, jelly, butter, bread, beans, hot dog, corn, peas, stew, spaghetti, mustard, sandwich, peanut butter, tuna fish, potatoes, hamburger, spinach, milk, etc.

TASK 158

Speech

Objective:

To label daily activities and objects encountered frequently.

Task:

Attach word labels to objects and activities. Talk to the child throughout the day and ask him to "Say _____" after you have labeled an object or activity. For example, in going out for play period you might label and ask the child to say: *coat, out, run, swing, sand, walk*, and *in*.

TASK 159

Speech

Objective:

**To respond to
the stimulus
"What is this?"**

Task:

Choose a familiar word which the child can
say easily (such as ball, cup, doll, etc.). Hold
the object in front of the child and point to
it. Say "What is this? John, say *ball.*" Reward a correct response. Repeat several
times using different objects. Then say
"What is this?" and wait for a response. If
the child names the object, provide a reward. If the child does not, repeat "What is
this?" and wait. If he still does not respond,
provide the cue "John, say *ball.*"

TASK 160

Speech

Objective:

**To increase the
number of objects
which the child
can label.**

Task:

Language field trip. Take the child to different environments in order to come in contact with different objects. Ask the child
"What is this?" for several objects. Provide
cues when necessary (for example, "John,
say *tree*").

Trips:

1. Parking lot (cars, buses, trucks, tires, lights).
2. Kitchen (foods, utensils, equipment).
3. Garden (plants, dirt, stones, bugs, worms,
   flowers).
4. Tool shed (rake, mower, shovel, saw, tractor).

TASK 161

Objective:

Vocabulary development, labeling, and sentences.

Speech

Task:

"Visitors" to the classroom. Bring into the classroom items of interest to children. (The more interested a child is in an object, the more anxious the child will be to acquire language relevant to it.) Children will label the item, label various parts of the item, identify the colors of the item, and identify what the item does. *Examples:* A frog. Labels: Frog, green, legs, feet, head, eyes, mouth. The frog sits. The frog jumps. The frog swims. The frog is wet. The frog feels slippery. The frog got away. The frog hopped around the room.

Other "visitors":
Kitten	Clown
Puppy	Motorcycle
Baby	Colored light display
Policeman	Drummer (or other musician)
Fireman	

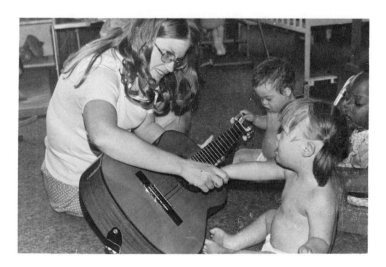

TASK 162

Objective:

Use of complete sentences and identification of action words.

Speech

Task:

Field trip. The purpose of the field trip is to answer the question "What is _____ doing?". The response to be elicited is: "_____ is _____." Walk around the school grounds or town where there are people (and animals) engaged in some form of activity. Ask the cue question and have children provide the appropriate response (with help initially as necessary). Examples of responses might include: "Jake is mowing"; "Bobby is running"; "The man is hammering"; "The pony is eating grass"; "The boy is raking"; "The lady is running"; "Mrs. Rains is sitting"; "Tom is washing the window"; "Nancy is riding a bike"; "The dog is barking"; "The bird is flying."

10 FINE MOTOR SKILLS

The tasks in the fine motor sequence are designed to develop grasping skills, manipulation skills, two-hand coordination, eye-hand coordination, and manual strength and dexterity. The fine motor section should generally be treated as a continuous sequence in which the performance of a given task is dependent upon the child's ability to perform the previous tasks in the sequence.

It is possible, however, for a child's curriculum to include three or four similar fine motor tasks simultaneously. It would not be inappropriate, for example, for a child to work during the same day on Task 169 (ringing a bell), Task 170 (pulling a string), and Task 171 (holding a mirror).

For some tasks, the performance of the task itself constitutes the acquisition of a necessary skill. For many other tasks, however, the task itself is of less importance than the abilities which it is designed to develop. That is, a child may have little practical use for the ability to squeeze water out of an eyedropper, but the activity is designed to improve the child's use of the thumb and forefinger in opposition and this ability is essential to many activities which are of practical value. The method by which the fine motor tasks are performed, then, is often more critical than the result of the task performance. It is suggested that the parent or teacher be particularly concerned with the methods a child uses to perform the tasks in this section. It is also important to note that for many of these tasks, repetition is important. That is, it is not sufficient for a child to perform a task one time and then move on to the next task. Rather, the child should continue to perform repetitions of the task as long as it remains a challenge to coordination, dexterity, or strength abilities. Three tasks—178, 179, and 209—are specifically designed to develop finger and hand strength and repetitions of these tasks are especially valuable.

The overall long-range objective of the fine motor sequence is the development of sufficient manual coordination, dexterity, and strength for the performance of such skills as dressing, writing, using utensils and implements and other manipulative skills essential for success in school work, vocational training, or independent living. The fine motor curriculum is applicable for children from infancy through adolescence, dependent upon the severity of the child's handicap.

TASK 163

Objective:

To stimulate the child to reach toward and grasp objects.

Grasping

Task:

Whenever the child is resting (naptime) or when the teacher is not able to work directly with the child, place attractive objects within the child's reach. Suspend a reachable object above the child and place other objects on the tummy or beside the child.

TASK 164

Objective:

To reach for an object with both hands.

Grasping

Task:

Hold a large toy which the child is attracted to in front of the child. When the child reaches with one hand, take the other hand in yours and place it on the object. When the child has both hands in contact with the object, move the object to the child.

TASK 165   **Grasping**

Objective: *Task:*

To reach toward   Hold an object that is attractive to the child
an object with   (this will vary with the individual) in front of
one hand.   and close to the child. If the child moves his
                            or her hand in the direction of the object,
                            move the object toward and give it to the
                            child. If there is no reaching movement at
                            all, physically manipulate the child's arm in
                            a reaching movement and simultaneously
                            move the object to the child. WORK WITH
                            BOTH HANDS. *Examples of objects:* doll,
                            ball, squeaky toy, rattle, bits of food.

TASK 166

Objective:

To reach for and grasp an object with both hands.

Grasping

Task:

Hold a large toy in front of the child. When the child reaches for it with two hands, give the child the toy. Help the child move the object toward his or her body if the child cannot hold it alone. Gradually reduce the amount of help you provide.

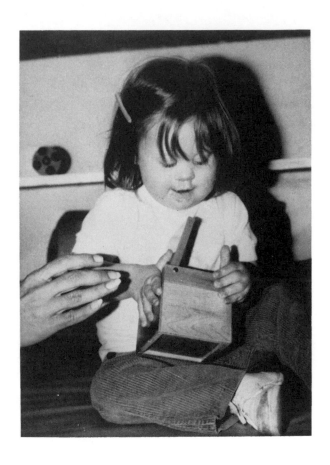

TASK 167   **Grasping**

Objective: *Task:*

To reach for an object with one hand.

Hold an object that is attractive to the child in front of and away from the child. When the child reaches out for the object and extends the arm at approximately full length, present the object to the child. WORK WITH BOTH HANDS.

TASK 168

Grasping

Objective:

To reach for and attempt to grasp an object with one hand.

Task:

Place the child's favorite toy or food within reach. When the child reaches for the object and makes an effort to pick it up, place your hand over the child's, bend the fingers into a grasping position, and assist the child in picking up the object and bringing it toward him or herself. Gradually reduce the amount of help you provide. WORK WITH BOTH HANDS.

TASK 169

Manipulation

Objective:

To grasp and manipulate a rattle and a bell.

Task:

Hold an object in front of the child. When the child grasps it and holds it, place your hand on the child's hand and manipulate the object appropriately. The child should use one hand at a time but should alternate hands. Gradually reduce the amount of help you provide. At task completion the child should manipulate the object independently.

Equipment:

1. rattle—shake the rattle to produce a sound
2. bell—hold a small bell by the handle and shake it to make it ring

TASK 170

Objective:

To pull a string to produce movement and sound.

Manipulation

Task:

Assist the child in grasping and pulling the string. A wooden spool or plastic ring may be attached to make grasping easier. The object should be attached to the wall or be otherwise stationary. Gradually withdraw assistance until the child can pull the string independently.

Equipment:

Any object which produces movement and/or sound when a string is pulled. *Examples* include:
1. Fisher-Price Bluebird
2. Mattel Farmer

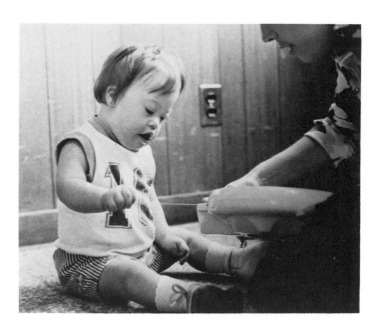

TASK 171

Grasping

Objective:

To grasp mirror by the handle.

Task:

Assist the child in grasping the handle of the mirror and holding it. Show the child that he or she can see his or her own image in the mirror.

TASK 172

Manipulation

Objective:

To grasp a tambourine in one hand and to shake the tambourine.

Task:

Hand the tambourine to the child and assist the child to grasp it in one hand. Hold the child's wrist and gently shake it so the tambourine produces a sound.

TASK 173

Manipulation

Objective:

To turn a knob or pull on dangling objects to produce movement.

Task:

Show the child how to manipulate the mobile by turning the knob or by pulling on the hanging objects. Assist the child in grasping and turning or pulling the knob. Gradually withdraw assistance and encourage the child to perform independently.

Equipment:

A mobile which moves freely when the knob is turned or when a dangling object is pulled or moved.

TASK 174

Manipulation

Objective:

**To pull a string
to make a pull toy
move across
the floor.**

Task:

Guide the child so that he or she grasps the string in one hand and pulls by bending the elbow or moving the body. Provide a reward. Encourage the child to pull the toy by him or herself.

Equipment:

A moving toy on the end of a string. Toys that produce sound when moved are preferable.

TASK 175

Manipulation

Objective:

**To push a small
wheel toy
across the floor.**

Task:

Assist the child in grasping a toy car or truck or other wheel toy and pushing it along the floor. Provide a reward. Withdraw assistance.

Equipment:

Any small wheel toy such as a car, truck, tractor, train.

TASK 176

Manipulation

Objective:

**To push on a
handle
to move a toy
across the floor.**

Task:

Assist the child in pushing the handle by moving an arm or the body. Withdraw assistance as soon as the child can move the toy alone. Provide a reward.

Equipment:

A push toy; a movable toy on the end of a handle.

TASK 177

Objective:

To lift, squeeze, spin, or wiggle in order to produce movement or sound.

Manipulation

Task:

Show the child how to manipulate a toy face and assist him in producing sounds and movements. Talk to the child as he or she is manipulating parts of the face and name the parts.

Equipment:

Kohner Bros. Busy Face.

TASK 178

Objective:

To curl fingers around and squeeze objects.

Manipulation

Task:

Hold an object in front of the child. When the child grasps it, place your hand over the child's hand(s) and squeeze the object to produce the desired effect. Gradually reduce the amount of assistance you give until the child is performing independently. Use one hand for some tasks, two hands for others.

1. Squeaky toy. Squeeze to produce a squeak (one hand).
2. Horn. Squeeze rubber bulb handle to produce a honk (two hands).
3. Sponge. Squeeze sponge soaked with water to cause water to run out (two hands).
4. Eye dropper. Squeeze bulb to fill with water and squeeze again to empty (one hand).
5. Baster. Squeeze bulb to fill with water and squeeze again to empty (two hands).

TASK 179

Objective:

To perform squeezing actions with the fingers and thumb for the purpose of developing muscular strength and oppositional coordination.

Manipulation

Task:

Have the child squeeze the objects listed below. Squeezing will produce a result (such as sound or squirting liquid). When the child produces the desired results, provide a reward. If the child cannot perform the squeezing behavior alone, provide manual assistance. Gradually withdraw your assistance. The child should gradually increase the number of squeezes per session until each squeezing task can be performed ten times in succession. Squeezing exercises should be performed several times each day.

1. Squeaky toys (rubber animals or dolls which make a noise). Alternate hands.

2. Horn (a tin horn with a rubber bulb). Use two hands initially. Use one hand if child has sufficient strength.
3. Sponges with water. Put a sponge in a bucket of water; lift the sponge out of the water; squeeze water from the sponge. Use two hands.
4. Eye droppers. Squeeze water out of a filled dropper using thumb and forefinger. Fill dropper by squeezing and releasing.
5. Mustard container (plastic bottle with spout). Squeeze with two hands to squirt water out.
6. Clay or play dough. Squeeze between two hands. Squeeze in one hand (alternate).

TASK 180

Manipulation

Objective:

To push, turn, dial, or slide in order to produce an effect.

Task:

Show the child how pushing, turning, dialing, or sliding causes the door on the equipment to pop open. Take the child's hand in yours and provide manual guidance so the child opens the doors. Provide a reward. Gradually withdraw assistance.

Equipment:

1. busy box
2. surprise box

TASK 181

Manipulation

Objective:

To pull, spin, grasp, push, dial, turn, roll, or slide to cause movement or sound.

Task:

Assist the child in appropriately manipulating the separate objects or the equipment. Reward enthusiastically each time the child properly succeeds in manipulating the equipment. Withdraw assistance.

Equipment:

1. Fisher-Price Activity Center
2. gym bar

TASK 182

Grasping

Objective:

To pick up and transfer objects from one location to another using the thumb in opposition to one or two fingers.

Task:

Have the child pick up an object and move it to a different location or place it in a container. Use progressively smaller objects as the child becomes more adept. Provide guidance so the child uses the thumb and one or two fingers to grasp the objects rather than using four fingers against the palm. Be sure that the child learns to finish a task once it has been started. Begin transferring two objects at a session and gradually increase to ten objects per session without interruption.

Progression of objects:
1. large blocks
2. small blocks
3. large beads
4. small beads
5. small pegs
6. pieces of cereal

TASK 183

Manipulation

Objective:

To use a spoon to transfer a substance from one container to another.

Task:

Place before the child a bowl containing flour or corn meal and an empty plate. Give the child a metal tablespoon. The child should grasp the spoon in one hand, scoop up a spoonful of the flour or corn meal, and transfer the substance to the paper plate. Demonstrate the task for the child and use manual guidance for assistance as necessary. When the task is mastered, progress to more difficult manipulations as follows:

1. Tablespoon. Move material from bowl to coffee can.
2. Tablespoon. Move material from plate to coffee can.
3. Metal teaspoon. Move material from plate to coffee can.

4. Metal teaspoon. Move material from plate to babyfood jar.
5. Small plastic spoon. Move material from plate to babyfood jar.

TASK 184

Manipulation

Objective:

To put the ball in the proper slot and then retrieve it.

Task:

Assist the child in putting the ball in the hole and retrieving it when it comes out. Withdraw assistance.

Equipment:

Curiosity Box

TASK 185

Manipulation

Objective:

To remove pegmen from slots and replace.

Task:

Show the child how to remove the pegmen from the holes in the object and then replace them. If the child does not perform appropriately, provide assistance. Provide a reward. Gradually remove assistance.

Equipment:

1. large pegs which fit loosely in a pegboard
2. peg toys such as those manufactured by Creative Playthings

TASK 186

Objective:

To develop hand-eye coordination and muscular control.

Manipulation

Task:

Assist the child in putting rings on a post and then removing them. Gradually reduce the amount of assistance you give.

Materials:

1. ring stand
2. large rings which fit loosely over a post

TASK 187

Objective:

To put shapes in the correct hole and retrieve from under the lid.

Manipulation

Task:

Assist the child in grasping blocks, selecting the correct slot and dropping the objects into the slot. Retrieve the blocks. The following pieces of equipment are listed in a progression from easiest to most difficult:

Equipment:

1. mailbox
2. tumble shapes box
3. Shape-O-Ball
4. any box with slots cut in shapes of square, circle, triangle, etc., and corresponding blocks

TASK 188

Manipulation

Objective:

To develop muscular control and hand-eye coordination by placing objects on other objects.

Task:

Have the child perform the following stacking operations. Begin with large-sized objects and move to smaller sizes. Begin with two or three objects and gradually increase to four, five, six, or more. These stacking operations should be performed three or four times each day until the child can stack several small blocks with ease. Reward stacking successes with praise or food.
Progression by difficulty:
1. large blocks (3 inches)
2. middle blocks (2 inches)
3. small blocks (1 inch)

TASK 189

Two-Hand Coordination

Objective:

To coordinate the use of two hands.

Task:

Place a bead, an M & M candy, or other small hard object inside one-half of a nesting egg. Place the other half of the egg on it so that the object is contained within the nesting egg. Shake to produce a rattling sound and give to the child. Assist the child if necessary to take the egg apart and retrieve the object. Repeat and withdraw assistance.

TASK 190

Two-Hand Coordination

Objective:

To develop two-hand coordination and muscular strength.

Task:

Have the child manipulate clay or play-dough between the hands. Use manual guidance as necessary and then withdraw. Have the child:
1. roll clay into a ball
2. roll clay into a snake
3. roll clay into three balls and make a snowman

Stress using two hands rather than one hand and the surface of a table.

TASK 191

Manipulation

Objective:

To push buttons, turn crank, push in drawer.

Task:

Using a Fisher-Price Cash Register, assist the child in pushing the buttons, turning the crank, pushing in the drawer. Provide a reward. Withdraw assistance.

TASK 192

Two-Hand Coordination

Objective:

To develop two-hand coordination and to learn a cranking motion. To develop muscular strength.

Task:

Teach the child to manipulate a jack-in-the-box successfully so that jack pops up. The child should hold the box with one arm and crank with the opposite hand. Initially the box may be partially cranked for the child so that one revolution or even a half revolution will cause jack to pop. Use manual guidance if necessary. When the child can successfully turn the crank several revolutions and work the box independently, you may teach the child how to push jack back inside and put the lid down.

TASK 193

Two-Hand Coordination

Objective:

To separate nesting items from one another. To place a small object into a larger one.

Task:

Show the child how to take the cups apart. Assist the child in performing the task. Provide a reward. Show the child how to put a small cup into a larger cup. Provide assistance and a reward. Gradually withdraw assistance.
Progression:
1. nesting boxes
2. nesting cups
3. nesting barrels
4. nesting eggs

TASK 194

Two-Hand Coordination

Objective:

To push down on the handle of the top to cause it to spin.

Task:

Show the child how the top works. Provide assistance as necessary and praise the child's success. Gradually withdraw assistance.

TASK 195

Two-Hand Coordination

Objective:

To twist ends of a shake-rattle in opposite directions to produce sound.

Task:

Show the child how the shake-rattle works. Assist the child in twisting the ends of the toy in two hands to produce a rattle sound. Reduce assistance until the child produces the sound independently.

Equipment:
shake-rattle by Creative Playthings

TASK 196   **Two-Hand Coordination**

Objective:

**To pull apart
popit beads
to develop
hand opposition
and coordination.**

Task:

Assist the child in holding one popit bead in
one hand and a second attached bead in the
other hand. Pull to separate the beads. Gradually reduce the amount of help you give
until the child can pull the beads apart independently. When the child can pop large
beads, begin to use smaller ones:
Progression:
1. strand of large, easy sliding popit beads
2. strand of smaller, more difficult beads

TASK 197   **Two-Hand Coordination**

Objective:

**To put popit
beads together to
develop hand
opposition and
coordination.**

Task:

Put popit beads together. Assist the child in
holding one bead in one hand, another bead
in the other hand, and pushing the two
beads together. Gradually reduce the
amount of help. When large, easy-to-insert
beads are mastered, begin to use smaller,
more difficult beads.

Equipment:

1. strand of large, easy-to-insert beads
2. strand of smaller, more difficult beads

TASK 198

Two-Hand Coordination

Objective:

To use hands in opposition; to develop grasping ability and finger strength.

Task:

Have the child hold one end of an 8½ x 11″ piece of paper in the right hand and the other end in the left hand. Have the child then move one hand forward while the other moves backward (toward the child) and continue moving the hands apart until the paper is torn into two pieces. Use manual guidance initially as necessary. Reward each tear. Use the following progression:
1. newspaper
2. tablet paper
3. heavy wrapping paper

TASK 199

Objective:

To pick up an object and strike a second object with the first.

Eye-Hand Coordination

Task:

Place a drum and a stick on the table or floor in front of the child. Demonstrate the cause-effect relationship of action and sound to the child by picking up the stick and striking the drum. Take the child's hand in your hand and pick up the stick and strike the drum. Encourage the child to repeat the activity independently.

Objects:

1. drum and stick
2. cymbals and stick
3. one pair of cymbals hit together

TASK 200

Objective:

Muscular development and hand-eye coordination.

Eye-Hand Coordination

Task:

The following may be used to increase the child's repertoire of manipulative skills. The child should be able to manipulate each of the following successfully:
1. surprise box
2. Playskool workbench (hit pegs with hammer)
3. busy box
4. manipulative board (several doors on a plywood board; each door has one of several assorted types of locks or catches; child must manipulate locks to open doors)
5. open door which has a push handle (the kind found on the inside of school doors)
6. open door with turn knob (common schoolroom and household knob)
7. turn light switch on and off

TASK 201   **Eye-Hand Coordination**

Objective:

To place an object in a slot (slot chart) for eye-hand coordination and finger dexterity.

Task:

Have the child place objects into a slot. Use the following progression:
1. 1″ disc and 3″ slot
2. ½″ disc and 1½″ slot
3. ½″ disc and 1″ slot
4. dime and piggy bank slot
5. large slot chart cards into large chart
6. small slot chart cards into small chart

Materials:

1. for discs for above use buttons, coins, poker chips
2. for slots use mayonnaise or baby food jars with slots in lids or piggy banks
3. slot charts are those produced by Ideal

TASK 202

Eye-Hand Coordination

Objective:

To put lids and tops on boxes and jars by coordinating eyes with both hands and learning to twist and push.

Task:

Have the child put lids on boxes and jars. Give the child the container and the proper lid. Use manual guidance as necessary. Reward correct performances.

Materials:

1. a small cardboard box (5″ x 5″) with a loose-fitting lid which is set on top of it
2. a shoebox and its lid; this requires the child to use two hands
3. a petfood can with a plastic top which can be put in place by pushing straight down on it with some force
4. a mayonnaise jar with a twist-on lid; initially, a single twist may be considered correct and rewarded; gradually demand more twisting until the child is putting the lid on securely
5. small bottles (such as a salt shaker) with twist-on lids

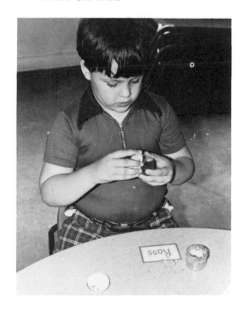

TASK 203

Eye-Hand Coordination

Objective:

To string beads of increasingly smaller dimensions to develop the ability to put a small object (needle) into a small hole.

Task:

Have the child place beads on a string. Gradually increase the number of beads per string from one to ten. Reward completion of each string. Use the following progression of items:

1. Large string (rawhide) with hard firm plastic end.
   a. large wooden beads
   b. large wooden spools
   c. smaller spools
   d. small wooden beads
   e. small spools
   f. macaroni

2. Package string with waxed end; shoe-
   string
   a. small wooden beads
   b. small spools
   c. noodles
3. Thread (heavy) with plastic needle
   a. glass beads
   b. buttons

TASK 204

Objective:

To pick up objects of different lengths and shapes and place them appropriately in a receptacle.

Eye-Hand Coordination

Task:

The following series of tasks can be used to improve the child's ability to pick up and transfer objects.

Progression:

1. fill a pegboard with wooden pegs 1″ diameter
2. fill a pegboard with wooden pegs of 2″ length and ¼″ diameter
3. fill a pegboard with wooden pegs of 1″ length and ¼″ diameter
4. fill a rubber pegboard with handle pegs
5. fill a small plastic pegboard with stacking pegs
6. fill a Chinese Checker board with marbles

TASK 205

Objective:

To pour liquid.

Eye-Hand Coordination

Task:

Place before the child a cup containing water and a large plastic tub. The child should pick up the cup containing the water and pour the water into the large plastic tub. Demonstrate the task for the child and use manual guidance for assistance as necessary. When the task is mastered, progress to more difficult manipulations as follows:

1. pour from a paper cup to a large plastic tub
2. pour from an eight ounce cup or glass to a tub

3. pour from a large glass into a pitcher
4. pour from a glass to another glass
5. pour from a pitcher into a large cup; small cup
6. pour from a pitcher through a funnel into a glass or cup

TASK 206

Objective:

To use implements for hammering, twisting, or turning.

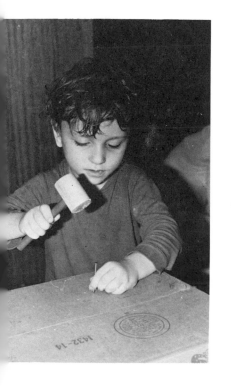

Eye-Hand Coordination

Task:

There are several manufactured items that can be used for this activity. The Playskool Busy Bench and Work Bench are very appropriate as well as homemade items such as a small section or 2″x4″ wood or a cardboard box.

Progression:

1. plastic hammers and screwdrivers and plastic nails and screws can be used initially to teach the motor act involved in working appropriately with tools
2. turn an empty cardboard box upside down and let the child hammer nails into the box; children can begin using wooden hammers and progress to adult hammers
3. after the child is able to manipulate a real hammer and nails allow the child to hammer the nails into a small piece of wood 2″x4″

TASK 207

Objective:

To improve finger-thumb opposition and finger dexterity.

Dexterity

Task:

The following activities can be performed using a deck of regular playing cards.
Progression:
1. 52 Pick-Up. Scatter the deck of cards on the floor and ask the child to pick up the cards and place them in a container. Initially, scatter five to ten cards and increase the number as the child's skill improves.
2. Card dealing. Place two or more flat containers, such as shoe box lids, on the table. Using four cards, demonstrate how to hold the four cards in the left hand and use the right hand to take the cards from the stack, one at a time and place in the boxes. The child should be taught to place one card in one box and the next card in the other box. As the child is able to manipulate four cards increase the number of cards which must be handled.

TASK 208

Objective:

To improve finger-thumb opposition and finger dexterity.

Dexterity

Task:

The following activities can be performed using ordinary hinged clothes pins.
Progression:
1. Give the child an empty cardboard box and a number of ordinary hinged clothes pins. Show the child how to open the clothes pins and place them on the sides of the cardboard box. Increase the

number of pins used as the child's ability improves.

2. Give the child an ordinary clothes hanger and a few clothes pins. Show the child how to place the clothes pins on the hanger. Increase the number of clothes pins and the number of hangers as the child's ability improves.

3. After the child is able to place clothes pins on a hanger, cut small pieces of material from an old sheet or towel. The fabric should be cut into small squares about 4" x 4". Show the child how to use a clothes pin to fasten the material to a clothes hanger.

TASK 209

Objective:

To increase strength of fingers and hands.

Strength

Task:

In order for a child to have the coordination to manipulate scissors or some type of writing implement it is important that the child have the strength to perform the movements involved in the activity. The following sequence is suggested for improving the child's hand strength:

1. Paper crumpling. Tear ordinary newspaper into small sections and show the child how to hold the paper in two hands and crumple it into a ball or wad. When the child is able to do this using two hands, have the child practice the skill using the right hand only then the left hand only.

2. Flour sifting. Obtain a flour sifter that has a squeeze handle. Place ½ cup of flour in

the sifter and show the child how to squeeze the handle to sift the flour. Initially, the child may use two hands if necessary. As skill increases have the child use the right hand only, then the left hand.

3. Tongs. Obtain a pair of tongs from a grocery or variety store. Several types are available, and you should purchase one type that requires using the entire hand to manipulate and one type that requires using your fingers much as you would when using scissors. Gather some small objects such as ABC blocks and show the child how to use the tongs to pick up the objects and transfer them to a container.

4. Tweezers. As the child completes the requirements in the task listed above, show the child how to use tweezers to pick up smaller objects and transfer them to a container.

TASK 210   **Dexterity**

Objective: *Task:*

To coordinate   There are many types of small stickers com-
different body   mercially available. The designs on the
parts in   stickers are colorful and appeal to children.
performing a task.   Purchase several of these sticker booklets
                          and teach the child to pick up the sticker
                          with one hand, lick the sticker, and paste the
                          sticker on a piece of paper. As the child be-
                          comes competent at placing a sticker on a
                          piece of paper, reduce the area and have the
                          child place the sticker in a small square.

TASK 211   **Dexterity**

Objective: *Task:*

To improve   Folding requires a great deal of finger coor-
finger dexterity   dination and skill. Children can improve
by folding   their coordination by learning how to fold
different objects.   the following objects:
                          1. towels
                          2. napkins or paper
                          3. socks
                          4. sheets

                          Note:
                          As the skill improves teach the child to fold in
                          halves and quarters.

TASK 212   **Dexterity**

Objective: *Task:*

To improve   Punch holes in a piece of tagboard or heavy
finger dexterity.   cardboard. Teach the child to pick up golf
                          tees one at a time from a container and place
                          the tees in the holes.

TASK 213

Objective:

To improve finger dexterity.

Dexterity

Task:

Listed below are several activities that adults perform routinely as a part of their daily living. These activities, however, are difficult for young children and involve a great deal of skill.

Progression:

1. Teach the child to slide a paper clip onto a piece of paper. Begin by using a large paper clip and sturdy paper (tagboard) and work down to a regular-sized paper clip and notebook paper.

2. Teach the child to pin a safety pin through a piece of material. Begin by using a large safety pin and work down to a regular-sized safety pin.

3. Teach the child how to tear a piece of scotch tape from a dispenser and to use the tape to tape two pieces of paper together.

4. Teach the child how to use a bottle of glue or a bottle of paste to put the substance on a piece of paper and stick it to another surface.

5. Give the child several objects and a rubber band. Show the child how to put the objects together using a rubber band.

6. Teach the child to punch holes in paper using a paper punch. This is a good activity for developing hand strength, and children find it enjoyable.

11 PERCEPTION

Many of the tasks included in the perception sequence are dependent upon fine motor abilities. It is difficult with many of these tasks to make a distinction between fine motor skills and perceptual skills. This distinction has been made, however, on the basis of the objective for the task. Tasks were considered to be primarily perceptual tasks if the objectives related to such concepts as sameness, compartmentalization, matching (shapes, sizes, colors or quantities), or various other visual or auditory discrimination skills.

The perception sequence is the most advanced of the areas presented. Because these tasks depend upon a certain level of fine motor and language ability as well as on perceptual abilities, children should not enter the perception curriculum until they have attained an appropriate developmental level. Depending upon the degree of the child's retardation, the tasks in this section should be appropriate for children between the ages of two years and eight years. Children who are only moderately retarded may be expected to progress through these tasks and to move on to a more academic preschool or school curriculum by the age of four or five years, while severely retarded children or perceptually handicapped children may never experience much success with the tasks in this section.

TASK 214

Objective:

**To put together
two like objects.**

Grouping

Task:

Place two paper plates on the table in front of the child with one plate beside the other. Say, "John, put the plates together," and at the same time pick up one plate and set it on top of the other place. Put the plates side by side again and repeat the instructions. If the child performs correctly, reward him. If he does not perform, repeat the instruction and manually assist him to perform the task. Provide a reward. Withdraw manual guidance as soon as possible. Continue to give imitative cues if necessary.

Repeat above using:

1. two napkins
2. two cups (one inside the other
3. two boxes (one inside the other)

TASK 215

Objective:

**To put together
three like objects.**

Grouping

Task:

Put three paper plates on the table side by side. Say, "Mary, put the plates together," and at the same time pick up one plate and put it on another and then put the third plate on the other two. Separate the plates. Repeat the instruction and reward the child if she performs correctly. Use imitative cues and manual guidance as necessary but withdraw manual assistance as soon as possible.

Repeat using:

1. three napkins
2. three cups
3. three boxes

TASK 216

Grouping

Objective:

To put like objects into a container which contains several like objects.

Task:

Place in front of the child a wide-mouthed glass jar which contains several (ten–twenty) beads. Also place in front of the child two beads identical to those in the jar. Say, "John, put the beads in the jar," and at the same time pick up one bead and drop it into the jar and then drop the second bead into the jar. Remove two beads and place them in front of the child. Repeat the instruction. Reward the child if he performs correctly. If he does not perform, repeat the instruction and use manual guidance to assist the child in performing the task. Withdraw manual guidance as soon as possible.

Repeat using:

1. blocks in a box
2. marbles in a can

When the child has mastered this task, repeat using three objects, four objects, and five objects.

TASK 217

Separating

Objective:

To separate two objects to make one pile into two piles.

Task:

Place in front of the child two paper plates, one on top of the other. Say, "Mary, take apart the plates," and at the same time perform the task. Restack the plates and repeat instructions. Reward a correct performance. Use manual guidance if necessary. Reward. Withdraw manual guidance. Repeat using:

1. two napkins
2. two cups (one inside the other)

When the child has mastered this task, repeat using three objects, four objects, and five objects.

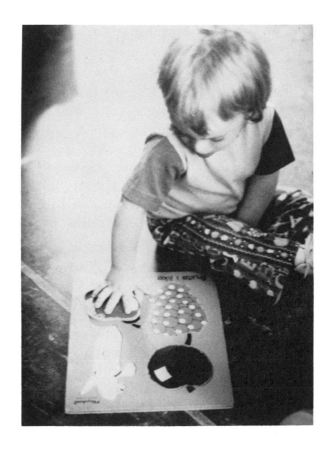

TASK 218

Puzzles

Objective:

To place the puzzle parts correctly in the puzzle.

Task:

Puzzles are an excellent means by which to teach the child order, assembly, fine motor coordination, and visual perception. Begin using them as the child is able to put one piece in a simple two- or three-piece puzzle. Progression:

1. one-piece puzzles; each piece has an individual slot
2. form board puzzles
3. five–nine-piece puzzles
4. ten or more piece puzzles
5. cardboard puzzles (sheets)
6. cardboard puzzles (boxes)

TASK 219   **Matching**

Objective: *Task:*

**To teach the child   The child should learn that the chair in the
different ways   living room is a chair, the chair in the dining
of matching   room is a chair, and the picture of a chair in
object to object.**   the magazine is a chair. The following
                       sequence is suggested for matching objects.
                       1. Match the object of a ball to the identical
                          object of a ball. Continue matching other
                          objects to like objects.
                       2. Match the object of a ball to a picture of a
                          ball. Continue matching other objects to
                          pictures of the objects.
                       3. Match the picture of a ball to another like
                          picture of a ball.
                       4. Match the picture of a ball to an "unlike"
                          picture of a ball.

TASK 220   **Grouping**

Objective: *Task:*

**To discriminate   Place in front of the child two paper plates,
between unlike   two napkins and two cups. Instruct the child
objects; to place   to put the plates together, put the napkins
like objects   together, and put the cups together. Provide
in a group.**   a reward. Assist as necessary and then with-
                       draw assistance. When the child performs
                       correctly consistently, increase the objects to
                       three of each, then four of each, and then to
                       several of each in unequal proportions.

TASK 221

Objective:

To discriminate between unlike objects; to place like objects in a group.

Grouping

Task:

Place a jar containing several beads and a box containing several blocks in front of the child. Then place before the child one bead and one block. Instruct the child to "Put the bead with the other beads and put the block with the other blocks." Demonstrate the task. Repeat the instructions. Reward a correct performance. If the child performs incorrectly or does not perform at all, repeat the instructions and assist the child to perform correctly. Provide a reward. When the child performs consistently, repeat using:
1. two beads and one block
2. two beads and two blocks
3. three beads and three blocks
4. several beads and blocks of unequal proportions

TASK 222

Objective:

To discriminate between unlike objects; to group like objects.

Grouping

Task:

Give the child three toy cars, three marbles, and two empty containers. Instruct the child to "Put all the cars in one box and all the marbles in the other box." Provide a reward. Assist the child as necessary and gradually withdraw assistance. When the child performs correctly consistently, present four cars and four marbles and then several cars and several marbles. When the child has mastered this task, repeat using three types of objects.

TASK 223

Matching

Objective:

To place objects of different shapes on outlines of the shapes.

Task:

Building blocks come in many different sizes and shapes. Purchase a set of blocks that are rectangles, squares, and triangles. On a piece of white tagboard trace the outline of these forms. Give the child blocks that match the traced images and ask the child to put the block on the outline that is the same as the block shape.
Progression:
1. fill in the tagboard images with the same color as the blocks
2. outline the tagboard images in the same color as the blocks but do not fill in
3. outline the tagboard images in black

TASK 224

Compartments

Objective:

To place two objects into containers with one object per container.

Task:

Give the child two beads and two containers (cans, jars, boxes). Instruct the child to place one bead in each container. Demonstrate. Reward all correct performances. Use manual guidance if necessary and then withdraw. If the child puts both beads in one container, say *"No"* and repeat your demonstration of the task. When the child has mastered the task, repeat using three, four, and five containers.

TASK 225

Compartments

Objective:

To place several objects into containers so that each container holds one object.

Task:

Place on the table six beads and an egg carton with six egg holes. Instruct the child to put one bead in each hole. Demonstrate. Repeat demonstration or use manual guidance if necessary. Reward all correct performances. When the child performs correctly consistently, use an egg carton with twelve holes and twelve beads.

TASK 226

Matching

Objective:

To group objects by color or to place objects on a surface by color.

Task:

This activity should begin using objects that are identical but of two different colors. Use two colors that are strongly contrasting such as red and blue. Give the child two objects of each color and have the child place the red objects in one box and the blue in another or the red objects on red paper and the blue on blue paper. As the child becomes proficient with two colors add a third and continue adding until the child is adept at eight colors.

Suggested objects:

1. match colored tagboard squares or pieces of construction paper
2. sort poker chips, plastic cars, plastic airplanes, checkers, marbles

3. sort and match checkers by sorting by red and black and then placing checkers on the appropriate squares of a checkerboard
4. sort and match marbles by sorting the various colors and then placing the marbles on the appropriate color of the Chinese Checkerboard
5. sort flannel board objects by color and group them on the flannel board in rows according to color

TASK 227

Objective:

**To match single
object cards to
a card containing
six or more
pictures (lotto).**

Matching

Task:

Once the child can successfully match two identical pictures, he or she may play several lotto games which involve matching skills. Lotto games may be purchased or they may be constructed as follows:

1. Divide a 6″ square piece of tagboard into nine 2″ sections and paste one picture (or sticker) in each of the nine squares.
2. Prepare a second piece of tagboard in the same manner and paste identical pictures (stickers) onto it.
3. Cut one of the tagboard cards into nine separate sections and leave the other whole.

The following lotto activities may be prepared and played (in progressive order of difficulty):

1. color lotto; match colored squares to lotto cards
2. animal lotto
3. common object lotto
4. black and white picture lotto (pictures of common objects in black and white rather than in color)
5. flower lotto
6. commercial lotto cards

TASK 228

Size

Objective:

To place "big" objects with other "big" objects and "small" objects with other "small" objects.

Task:

Place on the table one box which contains a few large (3″) blocks and one box which contains a few small (1″) blocks. Give the child one big block and one small block. Instruct him to put the big block with the other big blocks and put the small block with the other small blocks. Demonstrate and provide help if necessary. Provide a reward. As the child begins to respond correctly, interchange the positions of the containers.

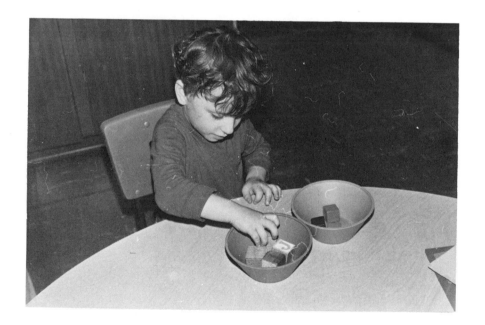

TASK 229

Size

Objective:

To discriminate between objects on the basis of size and to place like objects together.

Task:

Use two containers, one with "big" objects and one with "small" objects. Give the child two or three small objects and two or three big objects. Have the child put the small objects in the container with other small objects and the big objects in the container with other big objects.
Use:
1. blocks (3″ and 1″)
2. balls (baseball sized and golf ball sized of same color)
3. coins (50¢ piece and nickel)

TASK 230

Size

Objective:

To match lids to containers on the basis of size.

Task:

Have the child put the proper lid on a container. Use the following progression:
1. one box about 6″ square; two lids, one 6″ square and one 3″ square
2. one box 6″ square; two lids, one 6″ square and one 5″ square
3. one bottle 2″ in diameter; two lids, one 2″ in diameter, one 1″ in diameter
4. two bottles, one 2″ in diameter and one 1″ in diameter; two lids, one 2″ in diameter and one 1″ in diameter
5. two boxes, one 2″ square and one 1″ square; two lids, one 2″ square and one 1″ square

TASK 231

Size

Objective:

To fit together objects of different sizes by ascertaining the correct sequential size order.

Task:

Use the following progression:
1. Give the child two pieces, the largest and the smallest; show the child how to put the small one inside the large one; repeat.
2. Give the child 3 pieces, the largest, the middle sized, and the smallest; show the child how to put the smallest into the middle one and then the middle one into the large one; repeat.
3. Give the child the smallest piece and the next smallest piece; after the child has put those together, give the next smallest piece; continue handing the child pieces in order until the entire set is complete; repeat several times.
4. Give the child the three smallest pieces; let the child put them together by trial and error; repeat several times.
5. Give the child the four smallest pieces; let the child put them together by trial and error; repeat; repeat with five objects, six objects, and proceed to the whole set.

Materials:

nesting cups
nesting eggs
learning tower
nesting boxes

TASK 232

Objective:

To associate animal sounds with animal pictures and objects.

Sounds

Task:

Pictures and small animal objects should be obtained of farmyard animals and zoo animals that children can commonly identify. The child should be taught to match the animal object to the picture and to label the animal. Introduce the animal sounds so that the child learns to associate the sound with the picture of the animal and the object. The child should be able to:

1. produce the animal sound when shown picture of the animal
2. produce the animal sound when shown the object of the animal
3. select the correct picture or object when the animal sound is made by the teacher or another child

TASK 233

Objective:

To respond to a sound by performing a motor act.

Sounds

Task:

Use the following instruments to produce different sounds: bell, stick hitting the table, hands clapping. Tell the children that when they hear the bell they must run to the table. Ring the bell and have the children run to the table. Tell the children to sit in a chair when they hear the stick hit the table. Demonstrate. The objective of this task is to teach the child to associate different sounds with different acts. When the child has learned to run to the table hearing the bell or to sit in the chair when on hearing the sticks, add different sounds and require different responses.

TASK 234

Objective:

To follow instructions using a writing implement.

Writing

Task:

On the chalkboard, draw several shapes of common objects which the child can easily identify. Ask the child to place an X on the _____; draw a line from the _____ to the _____; circle the _____; underline the _____. When the child has mastered this task, repeat the commands but give the child a worksheet with objects and a crayon or pencil. As the child is able to associate labels of colors with crayons, ask the child to draw a red line from the _____ to the _____; a blue circle, etc.

TASK 235

Objective:

To develop the concept of body awareness.

Body Awareness

Task:

Play the Simon Says game involving movements which make use of body parts. Begin by having the children imitate your movements. This can be done later using peers as leaders or "Simon."

Movements:

1. raise your arm
2. touch your hair
3. touch the top of your head
4. touch your chin
5. touch your nose
6. touch your ear
7. stand up
8. sit down
9. turn around
10. touch the floor

When the child has mastered this task, repeat this task using ONLY verbal cues.

TASK 236

Objective:

To put together pictures of body parts.

Body Awareness

Task:

The teacher should cut out pictures of people from magazines, coloring books, catalogs, etc. Mount the pictures individually on heavy cardboard. Cut the pictures into sections that are logical—head, trunk, legs, arms. Show the child how to put the people together. Then give the child the materials and let him or her put the parts together.

TASK 237

Objective:

To recognize objects which are identical.

Matching

Task:

Give the child a box containing several pairs of objects such as two red cars, two blue cars, two yellow cars, two yellow airplanes, two red beads. From a similar assortment of objects, select one pair and an odd item and place them on the table (two red cars and one yellow airplane). Require the child to find those same items in the child's box and to place them on the table. Then ask the child to identify those items that are "the same."

TASK 238

Patterns

Objective:

To duplicate a visual pattern using objects.

Task:

On the table in front of the child place a pegboard which has a pattern filled in. Talk to the child about the pattern, "John, this is a fence. See how the edges of the board are all filled in." Take the child's hand so he can feel the pattern. Then give him a pegboard and pegs and ask him to make his board look like the other board.
Suggested patterns:
1. fence
2. X
3. cross
4. every other row

Note:

At a more advanced level, the child might duplicate a color pattern such as rows of alternating red and blue pegs.

TASK 239

Quantity

Objective:

To measure quantities of different substances.

Task:

Assemble several baby food jars or clear plastic glasses. Draw a ring around each jar or glass using a permanent magic marker. The lines should be drawn at different levels on the containers. Ask the child to pour water from a pitcher into the cup or glass and STOP when the water gets to the line. Using the same jars or glasses let the child use a spoon to transfer flour or corn meal from a bowl to the jar or glass. Again, ask the child to stop when the substance reaches the line.

TASK 240

Objective:

To place pictures in a logical sequence.

Time

Task:

The teacher should look through magazines, coloring books, and newspapers and cut out a series of pictures that tell some type of story—for example, coloring book pictures of a girl getting out of bed, eating breakfast, and getting on a bus. Cut the pictures out of the book and mount on three separate pieces of tagboard. Talk to the child about the action in the pictures and ask the child which picture happens first, second, and third. Continue this activity using different sets of pictures.

**A STEP-BY-STEP LEARNING GUIDE
FOR RETARDED INFANTS AND CHILDREN**

was composed in 12-point Photocomp Caledonia, leaded 2 points,
with display type in Helvetica;
printed offset on 66 Antique Pub. White paper stock;
adhesive bound, both hard cover and paper cover,
by Vail-Ballou Press, Inc., Binghamton, New York;
and published by

SYRACUSE UNIVERSITY PRESS
Syracuse, New York 13210